Walking in the Shadow

of a Schizophrenic

Power of Forgiveness

"Influence Through Writing"
Much Appreciation: Carmen
Brenda L. Moore
7/23/2021

By Brenda L. Moore

ROYSTON
Publishing

BK Royston Publishing
P. O. Box 4321
Jeffersonville, IN 47131
502-802-5385
http://www.bkroystonpublishing.com
bkroystonpublishing@gmail.com

Cover Design: Elite Cover Designs
Back Cover Photo: Briana Groves

ISBN-13: 978-1-955063-13-5

Printed in the United States of America

Acknowledgments and Dedications

First and foremost, I thank God the Father,

Jesus Christ our Lord and Savior, and the Holy Spirit

who I trust and love with all my heart.

I dedicate this book and give my heartfelt thanks to:

- ➢ Mrs. Susie Doswell, a woman of faith, mentor, and writer who also was my first inspiration for writing my story

- ➢ Loves of my life who are my children: Tameka, Knijel, and Aaron

- ➢ Grandchildren: Justin, Kaelin, Damond Jr., Diamond, Da'Janae, Amuri, Nathaniel, MaKaury, and Greatgrandchildren: Justin Jr. and Justice Marie

- ➢ Heina D. Moore, III (Dallas), this book would not exist without you

➤ In Memory of Derrick Pace—Son-in-law and

Braxton McGruder—Grandson

And thanks to Francheska White, my editor. for her phenomenal skills and wisdom.

Table of Contents

Introduction

I was settled, and I guess you could say at the climax of my life, for I had just begun my major in Christian Education. My hope was to become a teacher at a Christian Academy School or Bible University. I was a divorced single mother in my early twenties with two young daughters. Having come out of a five-year marriage from hell, a second walk down the aisle was never my intention.

In 1982, on the campus of the College of the Scriptures in Louisville, Kentucky, I met a man named Dallas. In a short time, I grew to love him as my soulmate. Without a doubt, he was the man, husband, and perfect stepfather for my two little daughters; however, I found out his persona wasn't as it appeared. Proximity does not necessarily mean "red flags" are visible.

About three months into the marriage, my daughters and I unknowingly became victims of a debilitating mental illness, chronic paranoid schizophrenia. Daily we tried to find the fortitude to survive living with this unfamiliar disease, being caught up in the crossfire of insanity, its longevity of psychosis, mean spirits, and inescapable shadows of schizophrenia. Not only was it awkward and distressing, but it also rapidly altered our lives. Although I felt more compelled to stay than to run, my heart pounded, for I knew there were no easy answers, quick fixes, or a scapegoat.

Our story exemplifies how, on a daily basis, my children and I maintained endurance through knowledge of the mental disease and the gravity of separating the illness from the person. Optimism, our connection with God, a consistent prayer life, and having an outlet was our means of survival. That is what made it possible to cope, as opposed to allowing the impact of the illness to consume and annihilate us. Along the way, our resilience was contingent on learning the art and power of forgiveness. Spurts of growth came from questioning my motives, being introspective, and at times pondering whether or not my marriage to Dallas was a Divine intervention.

It took fifteen years to pour out my soul in writing this book. I was uncertain of my readiness to subject myself to biases, the judgment of others, and, most important, I didn't want to expose my children to more pain. As painstaking and challenging as my life was with Dallas, the conflict and unconditional love caused me to become the woman I am today. I am encouraged to be forthcoming about who I am as a person, mother, and woman of God, the latter being of utmost importance. Over the years, I was motivated by a greater need to share our monstrous experience with a diverse audience in mental health facilities, individuals, and families plagued with schizophrenia mania or some mental similarities.

My expectation for this book is that my family involvement and journey with schizophrenia will be informative, transparent, connective, and supportive for all who can identify with our story. It gives you things to consider when engaging in a life-time relationship. It brings an awareness that we can seldom trust our human intellect and instincts when it comes to judging the character and intentions of a person. The Bible quotes are inspiring principles to take into consideration in dealing with yourself and others. The scriptures I've referenced tell us to carefully censor and guard our mind for it determines the direction in which we take in life; and that only the Spirit knows the inward thoughts of a person. Benjamin Franklin wisely said, *"An ounce of prevention is worth a pound of cure."* It is far better to put a stop to something than to try and correct it after the fact.

Chapter 1

Do Not Despise Small Beginnings

Growing older was an eye-opening experience and brought about many changes during my teen years of life. My confused upbringing and what I lacked in my childhood could very well have been repercussions for the decisions I made in my adolescent and adult relationships. My childhood was vague; however, I do recall a few good early years living with my aunt, Maymie Lee Dickerson.

My aunt owned a two-story house with a rustic look of salvaged barn wood. It was tall and overlooked a bountiful cherry tree with thick branches. As a child, my friends and I climbed the tree to lie down on the wide branches and sometimes sat on the limbs like it was a bench while dangling our legs. The first level of the house consisted of a front room and kitchen. The front room had a full-size bed, a potbelly stove, a dresser with a three-sided mirror, and a few wooden chairs scattered about the room. A few steps from the front room was a kitchen with an open floor plan but without the modern touches.

In the kitchen was an iron stove with four large burners covered with solid iron plates. There was a green wobbly wooden table with four weak straw chairs surrounding it. We kids were constantly told not to lean back or rock in those chairs. In one corner of the kitchen stood an antique china cabinet filled with beautiful china, and on top of the cabinet was a white ceramic bear with a large red heart on its side and the inscription, *"Fall City Bear."*

Adjacent to the antique cabinet was a tall chest that actually touched the brown spotted ceiling. Near the kitchen door leading outside was an unusually short, green icebox, known today as a refrigerator. I remember weekly visits by the "Ice Man" who brought a huge block of ice, which kept our food cold. He would place the ice inside the icebox and carefully empty the pan underneath that caught the melted water. Next to the kitchen door were steps leading to the second floor, which was a very eerie space. When climbing the stairs, each step would squeak as your foot touched step after step, and you could feel unleveled boards shift beneath your feet.

Upon reaching the landing of the second floor, complete darkness was interrupted by a glimmer of light from the two small windows located on each end of the long rectangle room. Depending on which window of the rectangle room we stood at, a good portion of the back or front yard could be seen. We were careful not to lean too hard on the fragile windows for fear we would break through and drop below. The long rectangle room contained a full-size bed and wall to wall antique toys, such as glass china tea sets, a small iron stove, rocking chairs, porcelain dolls, etc. Inside this same space was a second room, which was empty. A tiny window covered with a red cloth blocked illumination of light to the room. Narrow wooden, unleveled planks made up the flooring in this room. Streaks of light from the front room below would shine through the crevices of the loose planks. When we could play upstairs, each time my Aunt Maymie heard our footsteps and yelled, "Hey! Don't y'all go in her room, you'll fall through that floor." Somehow, I doubt these words ever reached the dictionary. Anyway, we understood.

The house was built so close to the street and sidewalk, conversations of people strolling down the sidewalk were clearly heard. Aunt Maymie, my three siblings, and I slept together in the four-post iron bed next to the front room window. The breeze from the open window and front door felt good on our faces. Many wonderful memories and conversations took place in that old iron bed. I was raised and had my early childhood memories in that house.

Like a revolving door, my mother would drop my siblings and me off in the care of my Aunt Maymie, and as quick as a vapor, she disappeared. However, inquisitive minds had questions and wanted to know the answers. One night, in his high pitch tone, my brother asked, "Aunt Maymie. Someone is upstairs. Who is that lady upstairs?" Silence fell over the room. We lay there anticipating an answer. Aunt Maymie' responded, "Don't yawl go in her room. Yawl gone fall through the floor." We never received an answer, only a command. You see, as far as we knew, it was only my Aunt and us kids, but secrets have a way of surfacing. Later, we learned that the person living on the second floor of my Aunt Maymie's home was no longer a mystery. It was our mother. What. Why. When. We were never informed. Besides finding out our mother was living upstairs, we also discovered there had been an addition to our family, a baby sister, and now there were five of us.

How could our mother reside in the same house with her biological children, and we do not know it, plus we have a baby sister who's cry we never heard. This entire scenario reminds me of a movie I saw years ago entitled *Flowers in the Attic*, in which the children lived in the attic of their grandmother's house while the mother lived downstairs. In the movie, the children were isolated and severely mistreated. I can certainly identify with the isolation those children experienced. Our mother lived closed off in the attic with a new baby, while all the rest of her children lived downstairs with an Aunt. As I was growing up, the norm seemed that children were kept in the dark about many family matters.

Even then, I don't remember having much contact with our mother. I am not certain when it took place, but my mother moved from my aunt's home to a house in a new subdivision named Lincoln Park on Silver Leaf Drive. All I know is my aunt unexpectedly passed the word to us that we were going to live with our mother. I'll always remember that cool morning when I was about ten years old. My middle sister and I wore new matching outfits, but different colors.

I wore a purple-flowered two-piece button-down blouse with mini-skirt and matching underpants; hers was the same, only it was pink. It was though we were dressed for the occasion. I walked down the narrow wet grassy path with my head bowed, feeling fast heart palpitations, despondent and confused at what was about to transpire. My stomach churned as I tried to envision the change. I had a dialogue with myself. "I don't know her…" At the age of ten, I felt I was being sent off to a bondless relationship. I was scared and didn't know what to expect. As I tried to make sense of the news, I thought about how I would miss the only person I knew who took care of me, my Aunt Maymie.

My siblings and I went to live with my mother, and shortly thereafter, we had two more additions. The cutest babies ever joined our family, which brought my mother's children to seven; five girls and two boys; namely, Sandra, Joe, Anna, Margie, Jamesetta, Adrian, and me.

Often, I was heartbroken for my aunt. She was a very caring, warm-hearted, spirited, and feeble soul. Behind her smile, her demeanor exhibited pain, loneliness, and deep secrets. It's my belief some of her sadness was due to not receiving the respect, care, and credit deserved for all those years she washed, ironed, cooked, and gave of her time to her nieces and nephews.

Weekend visits with my aunt came and went quickly. No sooner than we arrived, seems it was time to say goodbye. Whenever it was time to leave, my stomach groaned, and my eyes filled with tears as the cab drove down the dusty graveled road. I'm not certain if it was more painful to leave her or the fact I was returning to an unhappy place. We kept our necks turned and sometimes faces pressed against the windows of the Yellow Cab as we tried to keep the view of her waving goodbye while standing on the front wooden porch.

Life with my mother, whom we call "*Mu-ah,*" was like living in an amusement park and not in a good way. Sporadically there were moments of giggling and fun, but the majority of those times were when we were playing with our neighbors. Other times life with our mother resembled a merry-go-round or a roller coaster ride. Her moods were up and down. It was also like being in a horror house and never knowing what would transpire. I tried effortlessly to please her, to make her feel my heart, and be proud of me. Occasionally, I received a compliment for cleaning the house and "A" papers from school; in fact, she filed them away. I think in their own way, my siblings tried to please her as well.

My mother had her last child at age 45. I heard my baby brother's cry in the middle of the night and sprung from my bed to change his diaper, gave him a bottle, and whatever else was needed. Not only did I love such a handsome fellow, I felt good doing this for Mu-ah while she slept. One particular day, I had babysat my brother most of the day, and as I walked out the front door to get some fresh air, this car was zooming by. I recognized my mother in the car and yelled to her if I could go to a friend's house. An unfamiliar voice yelled back, "She said, take the baby with you." I was quite familiar with this picture. My Aunt Maymie had gone through this as well. Of course, I dressed my brother, which I loved doing, and took him along with me. Neighbors who frequently saw me thought my brother was mine. Perhaps this is one reason why there will always be a place in my heart for children who are babysitters and a co-parent for their siblings because they miss the adventures of childhood.

My mother lacked communication skills with her children. I can still hear her voice when she was upset with us, "You mother f---" "Son of a b---" "I brought your ass into this world, and I'll take you out..." What had my siblings and I done to be accosted with such names? She also threatened to send us to a home or Pee Wee Valley, which was a women's prison. And she would add, "They cut off your hair in there." I can relate to pictures of a child sitting in a corner with a bowed head retreating from it all.

One day a friend of mine wanted me to go to the park. I stood behind the kitchen wall, looking off into the living room, watching Mu-ah as she lay on the couch. Numerous times, I'd peek around the corner at her and then fall back. It literally took thirty-minutes to get up enough nerve to ask if I could go with my friend to Newburg Park. What should have been comfortable for any child was like a chore to me. It took time and effort to ask anything of her. My body occasionally went through moments of fear and withdrawal.

We were also whipped, and many times it was undeserved. I hardened and refused to cry, so my beatings were worse. Her tactic for me was, "You won't cry, then I will whip harder and longer, oh, you will cry." Extension cords, long slim tree limbs that wrapped around your legs, belts, shoes, anything she could lay hands on was used to whip us. During one whipping, I said respectfully, yet boldly, "I want to go to the home." Anywhere was better than living with her. The unexpected outburst blew her mind. I actually took her up on her own offer and called her bluff. I guess she never expected to hear those words from me. This was one of those situations where someone has made a statement or promise, now they are forced to honor it.

Mu-ah phoned my grandmother and told her what happened. My grandmother called my Aunt Maymie, who lived with us but was unaware of what happened. Auntie pleaded with me not to go. But I had enough and was ready to leave. Mu-ah kept me home from school, but nothing ever came of sending me away. I cornered my aunt in her bedroom one day and asked why Mu-ah was so mean to me. My aunt replied, "You look so much like her, and I think she feels you are going to be like her." Whatever that meant.

A neighbor or friend knocking at our door always brought excitement for me. It meant company for Mu-ah, and these times were our peace because mother's focus was deterred from us kids. I visited my friend's homes and observed their relationships with their parents. I longed to have their mother as my parent, in fact, anyone's mother but mine.

Soon after Mu-ah passed, her mother came to our house. At one time, she was a beautiful blues singer, and according to my Aunt Maymie, she was blinded at a young age. My grandmother never appeared to have much of a relationship with my mother or us. While she was at our house, she yelled at me, "You killed her as sure as I am sitting here, when you told her you wanted to go to a home." In disbelief, I turned and looked at my grandmother, never breathing a word, then I left out the door.

When my siblings and I were older, occasionally, we reminisced and discussed the past. It never ceased to amaze me how each of us had unfamiliar memories and different perspectives about Mu-ah and our upbringing. Some moments I felt I hated her; I refused to neither entertain the negativity nor allow the thought to linger in my head. Subconsciously, I knew I didn't hate her; I hated what she had done and, at times, wanted to be free of her.

When I was a child, I didn't know anything about forgiveness. It wasn't until I became a Christian that I reflected on my life, and what might have caused Mu-ah's unhappiness to enable me to forgive her. I learned and understood happiness to be circumstantial, co-dependent, focused on materialism, money, popularity, someone, praises of others, and is contingent on "ifs." Happiness depends on what today or tomorrow brings when, in reality, no one can be the basis of a person's happiness. We were siblings of five different fathers. She married my older sister's father, and we all somehow took on his name. My assumption was perhaps neither of these men returned the love she had for them, especially my father.

The rumor was, she found out he had another woman who he put through nursing school, which left my mother feeling despair and betrayal. My mother's father was unknown (sounds familiar), and neither was she certain if my grandmother was her biological mother. Could family instability and broken relationships possibly be an underlining reason for my unfulfilled life?

I witnessed my own circle of friends speak of how much they hated their children's father, and the children were treated accordingly as if the children had a choice to be born. Maybe this explains Mu-ah's irritability and abusive behavior, especially toward one of my sisters. In my opinion, my sister looked so much like our father, and perhaps this was a constant annoying reminder to our mother.

One thing I can say is, we never wanted for food, and so this incident was out of the norm. Nonetheless, I recalled the time my siblings and I were in hot water because someone ate the last of the peanut butter. Our home had concrete floors overlaid with tile. You could hear a pin drop as we stood around to hear the judge and jury's (Mu-ah's) verdict regarding the guilty party. I'm not certain if one of us told, or my sister fearfully admitted she ate the peanut butter. What happened next was the most memorable. Ma-uh picked up my sister and slammed her to the floor, which resulted in some type of leg injury. It was jaw-dropping. Silently we stood petrified while listening to my sister crying with our eyes bulging from disbelief at what our mother had just done.

From that day to the present-day my sister has a physical scar on her leg, reminding her of the incident. Even worse, her heart was scarred. It was a bitter cup for me to drink from when our mother left a terrifying image in the mind of my sister when she perceived me as a reflection of our mother's evil shortcomings. I look and have a voice tone like our mother. Although this sister and I were the ones who suffered the brunt of harsh whippings over all our other siblings, for years, she thought I should understand her actions better.

One day, when I was in my late thirties, this same sister asked to come to my apartment and talk. While I sat on the living room floor doing my hair, I could hear footsteps and whimpering. There was a rattling of the doorknob as if someone was trying to open the door, then I heard a "stabbing scream" and thumping of swift footsteps down the stairs. I heard our friend yell my sister's name. A hurt feeling and confusion came over me as I thought how to handle the situation, so, instantly, I asked God if I should go after her. A soft voice said, *"No. She has to do this on her own."* I waited. There was silence for a while, and then again, I heard voices outside my apartment door. Our friend coerced my sister back up the steps, and this time the door opened. It took about an hour to recognize my sister had arrived and for her to get up the courage to enter my apartment. She walked down the long hallway before entering the dining area while reaching for a. light switch. My sister asked, *"Where is the light switch?"* I didn't have a chance to respond before the room became dark. She had found it. The only beam of light came from the parking streetlamp, dimly showing through the living room window. Next, I heard a chair being drug across the floor. Most startling was her next move. My sister turned the chair away from me and faced the wall. My heart cried. She could not look at me. I kept my words and motions in tack. The conversation began with my sister expressing her feelings. Following our conversation, my sister left out my door the same way she came, in the dark.

Even though at the time nothing was resolved, I was assured the capacity for healing was there. Driving by my sister's home brought about sentimental moods. Although I wanted to stop for a visit, I felt my presence might rehash old memories. I rested in the thought that there are problems <u>only</u> God can breakthrough. I, too, was a child trying to find my way through life, so how was I the blame? It wasn't until I planned a women's program that I got my answer. The theme was *When Helping You is Hurting Me.* I asked the women of our Dorcas Circle to give a testimony of an experience when helping someone became unhealthy for them.

I gave my testimony of how I felt about the relationship with my sister, and that day I vowed to shed my last tears and leave it in God's hand. For years it was a heavy and lonely burden to carry. I observed the judgment of others because of hearsay. I recognized and owned the fact that it wasn't me. It was the past that came between us, and I refused to allow it to fester in my spirit. God helps us see people in a different light, no matter how they have hurt or wronged us. I would never try to get in God's business nor think for Him.

Years after Mu-ah passed, I went through a period when I acted like a mediator of wisdom as to why God took Mu-ah. I, not God, concluded that He took Mu-ah so my siblings and I could live. I thought, what if we had lived out our adolescent years with our mother and remained in such a negative environment. I wondered how would we have turned out? I told myself we needed to be liberated to find our identity, to make our own mistakes free from critical judgment, to explore life, and accept we were worthy of more than how we were treated.

Last but not least, I shared with certain mentors and my church family that I could not make sense of how after Mu-ah's death, six children ages two through seventeen, were allowed to remain in a house with a seventy-two-year-old disabled aunt and with little or no interference from Child Protective Services. Afterward, this mysterious thought, I saw CPS as a negative for us. It could have been worse. What if we were placed in the legal system as orphans? We could have been separated and even placed in an abusive foster family.

On the contrary, there were good qualities about Mu-ah. She was smart, energetic, good looking, shaped like a "brick house," and she was an immaculate, sharp dresser. Her favorite color was black, and she wore it well. Her shoes were kept in the original boxes and placed neatly in her closet. She was a unique, excellent cook who made meals and desserts I will never enjoy again. According to acquaintances and my Aunt Maymie, Mu-ah was a great dancer, especially the Jitterbug. She worked constantly and was a hard worker.

I remember Mu-ah speak of standing on her feet while working at a place on Walnut Street, which was a thriving African American business district from the '20s to '50s in Louisville, KY. I witnessed firsthand her impeccable work ethics. Back in the day, our kitchen was her workplace. She was referred to as the "Queen of Marcel

Curling Irons." Mu-ah started early each morning and stood till late evening styling hair. Every now and then, she sat on the tall stool behind her. She would place her hand on her hip, bending from side to side to relieve the pain from her back. Hairdressing was how she provided for the family. On holidays such as Easter, Thanksgiving, and Christmas, she put in extra hours. As a single parent, times were hard and especially at Christmas. Mu-ah called us in the living room. Her countenance was the appearance of sternness of which we were accustomed. Only this time, it wasn't something we had done; it was a look of a heavy heart. She told us she could not afford to give us Christmas gifts, not even purchase a tree. However, she did not give up. Mu-ah continued styling hair and went to the Bingo Hall with the intent to win money to ensure we had something for the holiday. With a streak of luck, she won $300.00. Back then, that amount of cash could purchase much. She bought an artificial white Christmas tree, decorated it with gold ornaments, and placed a tri-color light rotating wheel underneath that turned the three different colors. Christmas morning, I walked into the living room, and under the tree was a gold bike. I just knew this bike was for my brother or one of my sisters. It was for me. My siblings and I had the best Christmas that year.

Mother taught me how to be a self-sufficient, independent person who could earn what I wanted. My older sister, Sandra, definitely inherited Mu-ah's work ethics. One Christmas, a few years later, Sandra lifted some of the burdens. She taught us how to make taffy candy to sell. After the taffy was cooked, my sibling's job was to drop in food coloring in the pot, pull the taffy until it thickened, shape the pieces, and wrap them in wax paper. Sandra told us the amount to charge and sent us door to door to sell the candy. We were excited to do so. I loved her for that. Left to raise ourselves, I contribute our survival skills to my mother. Working was in our blood.

In spite of despondency in our home and my relationship with Mu-ah, honestly, I believed she loved us as much as she could. She was my God-given mother, and I chose to respect her. Although times with her were bittersweet, I focused on "teachable moments" and particular experiences. I was taught to respect my elders, to use manners, to keep my body clean, and to keep a clean house. I cooked daily for my babies because I ate hot meals with dessert daily. She taught me little significant tips such as cleaning up while preparing a meal to alleviate a lot of mess and to always wear clean undergarments to bed, "You never know when you may get sick and have to go to the hospital," she would say. *"Honor your father and your mother, so that you may live long in the land the LORD your God is giving you. Exodus 20:12 (NIV)* The command of God was not conditional.

Retained knowledge from her was a steppingstone for me to choose a career and added stability to my teenage and adolescent years.

I took notes from her parental mistakes by promising myself I would never repeat them when raising my children. Left parentless at the age of fifteen, I had alternatives. I could have allowed myself to fall through the cracks or to make sure I lived a productive life. Many days I wished Mu-ah had lived to see my successes and how my life evolved. In my heart, I know our relationship would have been different. There are moments when I am in awe at the relationships some women have with their mothers, and I long for Mu-ah's conversation. However, I'm glad God is in control, and His Almighty hand was on my siblings and me.

The Controller

When the world seemly is taking control

Remember, God holds the remote

When your mother and father forsake you

Remember, God has the remote

When family and friends can't be found

Remember, God has the remote

Essentials of life are scarce

Remember, God has the remote

When your faith is at the bottom of the barrel

Remember, God has the remote

When your peace is fading

Remember, God has the remote

God is the Controller

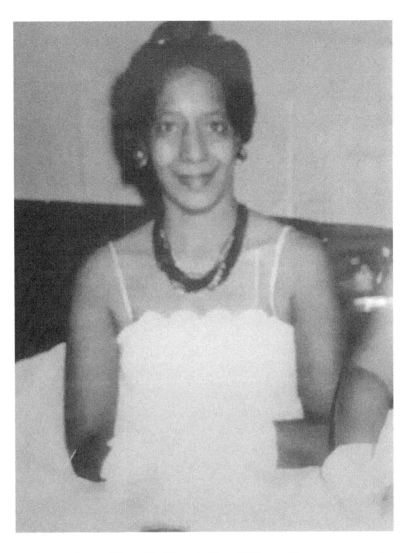

My mother, (Mu-ah), Fannie Lee Wilson Groves, passed

from this life at an early age of 47 years old, at 7 pm,

Saturday morning, April 17, 1971.

Chapter 2

Out of the Frying Pan into the Skillet

At the early age of fifteen, family was a matter of importance to me—the thought of having my own family brought a spirit of tranquility. I envisioned having a 'happily ever after' marriage. Needless to say, what I envisioned was not how my first encounter with marriage unfolded. My first mistake was that I lived with my boyfriend, Edward.

On a Sunday morning, the Sunday school teacher of the New Convert Class commented on the word *"fornication"* and explained that living together was wrong. A flush came over me as if the teacher could see I stood guilty. I reflected on my situation and wanted to right my wrong. My rationale was that it was okay because I loved Edward, and he's the father of my child. After much self-dialogue and numerous talks with Edward, we chose to rectify our situation by getting married. I was eighteen, and Edward was twenty-two years old when we got married.

There was no 'happily ever after' for us. Our relationship was already toxic while dating, and I should not have expected anything different in the marriage. What followed was violent emotions, name-calling, and unrest. Day and night, I immediately knew a misunderstood word or an out of place object would cause a violent eruption from my husband wherein I was slapped, hit, my hair literally pulled from the follicles, threats of putting me out, and adultery, all of which was not what I envisioned for my marriage. In fact, danger signs were already there; and my expectations of anything different were unrealistic.

After two separations and five years of hell, reality set in that marriage to Edward was never going to be a happy, lasting union. Through personal experience, I truly understood what women meant when they said, *"divorce felt like a death."* I moved on with our two daughters after the divorce, but the desire for a complete family was still a part of me. I learned the hard way that children plus love alone are never a basis for marriage. "Two wrongs don't make a right."

A New Phase in My Life

Still in my early twenties and during this new phase in life, occasionally, I had male friends with whom I would engage in conversation. However, it was nothing serious for dating was of no interest to me. I had gotten used to single life again. My priorities were God, my daughters, and my education. Don't let anyone fool you, singleness comes with a whole new set of issues. Single or married people will always have their *"assumptions."* I moved into an apartment complex where many of my neighbors were new, and some were old acquaintances who couldn't grasp my living arrangements, and so the gossip began. I consider this to be a typical behavior when others prefer a different lifestyle. Then one day, I was approached by a guy who lived adjacent to my apartment, who had an outspoken personality. One day on my way to the college, he walked up beside me, boldly and began questioning me.

"Can I ask you something?"

"Yes, what is it?" I answered.

"I heard you were a Lesbian. Are you?"

I chuckled and then became just as blunt, "It's like this, if I have to be called a lesbian because I don't have every Tom, Dick, and Harry running in and out of my home, then so be it. I know who I am, and I have two daughters, of which I need to be an example."

News circulated around the neighborhood that I must be a lesbian because men were never seen coming in and out of my apartment. That ended the conversation until we departed one another's company. I couldn't get mad, and I respected him for wanting to know the facts.

I was young, attractive, goal-oriented, knew what I wanted to do career-wise, and I was still family-oriented.

Although skeptical, I hadn't taken getting married again out of the picture altogether. If there was to be a second time around for me, I didn't want to make another or the same mistake. It had to be different from my first marriage. I looked at my first husband as being a person I would spend my life with, ironically never did I see him as being my soul mate.

Moving On

Following my Baptism and overcoming the disappointment of a bad marriage, I decided I wanted to make some changes in my life. I wanted to learn more about God and this new life in which I had committed myself. I decided to attend Bible College with a goal to become a teacher in a Christian school. Two years later, I attended The College of the Scriptures (COS), a Bible College in Kentucky that had a unique origin dating back to 1945.

Stemming from slavery, Blacks were looked upon and treated as incapable of learning and not given the privilege of becoming scholars, educators, and instructors. The COS was birthed during a period when Blacks were not allowed to integrate with White students on University campuses. The Bible College was started by a White Christian gentleman/Pastor who was compassionate to the needs of a school for Blacks to attend. He wanted to offer education in the field of ministry to graduate preachers, ministers, evangelists, and missionaries. His goal was for those graduates to provide leadership in the Black community and start Black churches in Urban communities all over the United States.

The College of the Scriptures consists of five buildings sitting on seven acres of land surrounded by clusters of beautiful trees throughout the campus. The men resided in a building for a dorm and a women had access to a House Trailer for a dorm. There was a library named after Samuel Buckner and an unfinished cafeteria/maintenance and housing quarters. The Maxey Building, which was named after the gentlemen who started the school, housed classrooms, business offices, Fellowship Hall and a Chapel. Everyone on the college campus was warm and inviting. It was like having an extended family for which I was not accustomed. This was the place where I gained more insight into living a purposeful life and engaging with people who cared about me. This campus also presented two life-changing events for me. First, in 1982 I received an Associate Degree in Christian Education. Second, I met the next man in my life.

Flashy and Classy

On a beautiful spring day in 1981, while on my way to class, I noticed a shiny cardinal red Camaro pull into a parking spot on campus. An attractive young man got out of the car. He was of short stature with a muscular small body frame, bronze skin, and neatly groomed black hair with a radiant smile. He approached me and introduced himself as Heina Dallas Moore, III, and we departed ways. Shortly following our greeting, he became a part of the student body but lived off-campus.

Over time, Dallas and I frequently conversed which revealed more about him. Like his father, Dallas said he joined the military in 1978 with the intention of making it a lifetime career and devoting his life to serve in the US Army. While enlisted, Dallas was a truck driver for the troops and a Colonel, platoon leader, and became an expert M16 marksman. He also aspired to be an Air-Born Ranger. Never did I assume our occasionally running into one another would lead up to any more than a casual conversation and maybe a possible friendship. More personal conversations showed me we had many things in common. When Dallas spoke of his childhood, he recalled more unpleasant experiences and memories than good and said he didn't have a family. Often, he expressed feelings of rejection, isolation, and being misunderstood.

I also talked about my childhood and divorce. Since I always had my two beautiful young daughters with me, Dallas assumed I was a mother, and he accepted my children too. Another common attribute we shared was care and courtesy. During my work hours in the library, he made it a point to stop in to say hello. In the fellowship hall, he would meet me at the coffee table and tell me that coffee was bad for me. In the chapel, he appeared. I soon figured out he had a watchful eye. On Thursday mornings during worship service, he took it for granted that he could sit by me.

In class, Dallas never took notes or used a tape recorder. His comprehension and understanding were profound. His brain was like a sponge, and he retained information like a computer. He could have easily instructed the class. He had the skills of an etymologist.

Dallas knew the meaning, could illustrate an example, and sometimes knew the root word of just about any word he was given. Needless to say, he made straight A's in Greek. I was attracted to his mind. I admired a man of few words, how he listened, and when he spoke, knowledge flowed from his lips. I am drawn to intellectual men.

On a Thursday following chapel service, the Dean of Women called me into her office. She was blunt and wasted no time asking, "Are you getting married?" Blown away at the question, it took a moment to digest before I responded, "No. Why?" I asked. Looking me dead in the eye, she claimed, "Well, Dallas is going around telling people that he is going to marry you." At a loss for words, my lower jaw expanded. My response was, "He's crazy.

"Seeing is better than hearing." African Proverb

Chapter 3

He Who Finds a Wife Finds a Good Thing

"All that glitters is not gold."

Dallas and I looked good and were good together. As a couple, we participated in most activities, attended after school events, programs, and rallies. Our first date was attending the College of the Scriptures Sweetheart Banquet that was held at a restaurant. Dallas suggested we dress alike and so he took me shopping. I wore a beautiful black and yellow dress that created a silhouette outline of my body without being tight. The bodice was a pastel yellow with tiny black dots that extended to a peplum to accent my waist, and the skirt was solid black. I topped my outfit off with yellow and black accessories and black heels. Dallas gave me a yellow carnation corsage with the petals trimmed in black. He wore a black suit with a yellow shirt, the same color as the bodice of my dress, and a yellow tie with tiny black polka dots. He was a lover of suits and was a sharp dresser. A Christian, intellectual, sharp dresser, three pluses; he was definitely my kind of man.

During our courtship, we enjoyed picnicking, playing games, and laughing with each other. Grocery and clothes shopping were always fun and pleasant for the kids as well. Sunday worship and mid-week services was not a question. Dallas was involved in the services and had many spiritual gifts, especially the gift of praying. My daughters, Dallas, and I prayed together. Together we read and studied the Bible. While lying across the bed, he and I would read a different book and then discuss the highlights of what was read. We loved being together.

For an unwed couple, intimacy came easy for us. Love is not all sex. It is an appetite, hunger, and thirst for enjoying your partner's company. Love is being content with companionship, sitting and holding each other, and holding hands in public. Love is lavishing each other's company for hours, taking turns listening to one another's thoughts, beliefs, goals, dreams, and not growing tired and sometimes falling asleep. Love is serene moments sitting together on the bank of the river, on a park bench observing God's creation. Love is traveling together in a car, not saying a word, yet knowing everything is okay.

Dallas said to me one day while we were together, "I just got baptized and went right back into sexual activity, and I didn't feel comfortable with what I was doing. I came out of a lascivious relationship and clubbing. I'm looking for something different. I don't want to go backward. I saw you, and it was something different."

Honestly, it was not always easy. There were principles and boundaries that kept us under control. In our relationship, there was a mutual respect for each other and for God. A priority on my list of wants in my next relationship was for a man to love God as I did and earnestly wanted to be obedient to His will. I was not only drawn to Dallas's intellect but his spirituality. We truly acted like a married couple without living together and the intimacy of having sex. One year later, Dallas proposed. I was more than ready to say yes. Apparently, he wasn't crazy after all. We were married on March 2, 1982, in the chapel at the College of the Scriptures.

Strong Ties

Dallas was either watching my body language or intuitive because some days after grocery shopping, he politely said, "Brenda, you're tired, go on upstairs and lie down, the kids and I will put up the groceries." I appreciated those little moments, and so occasionally, I rewarded him. While on a shopping spree, I made it a point to look for some sexy negligee to keep life and excitement in our marriage and to show appreciation for who he was in my and the kid's life.

One of Dallas's favorite things to do was to shop and surprise the girls and me. Interestingly, just like his impeccable taste in dressing, his taste in female clothing was spot on. We were a strong couple, preferring togetherness, family functions, or activities. Taking care of business was consistent even after marriage.

Dallas was a disabled veteran, and I worked part-time at the Bible College and the Laubach Literacy Program located at Spalding University. We had a unique household system. On paydays, Dallas and I sat at the kitchen table and laid both incomes out. Tithes were always deducted first, and then we prioritized the bills from major to minor, and the remaining money was split between the two of us. If the girls had a need, there was no discussion because their needs were met. Although I had my share, it was nothing for Dallas to ask if I needed anything and would often add a few more dollars to my stash. I remember Pastor Henry Johnson saying, "You treat your wife like a queen; she will treat you like a king." I loved Dallas for the respect and concern he had for my children and me.

One year, I participated in the Annual Kentuckiana Women's Retreat (ACWR). This organization of God's women originally took place at the North 35th Street Church of Christ in Louisville, Kentucky. It was under coordinators Janet Wilson and Susie Doswell. The purpose of ACWR ministry was to bring together women of color so we could share our pain, trials, and spiritual gifts to encourage and lift one another. Of course, all women were invited. The retreat started with twenty women, and over the years, the numbers increased to over 200 women from various cultures, states, and countries. Dallas was supportive of this ministry and any Christian function or work in which I was involved. He made sure I had the essentials on out-of-town trips. Every trip, he sent me off with a spirit of love, which added beauty to our relationship. I enjoyed being away, but I could hardly wait to get back home to his arms, his smile, and to hear his gut laugh when he found something amusing.

In times of crisis, we maintained a healthy attitude. One particular crisis was in January 2008 during a gruesome ice storm. We awaken one morning, the house was freezing, there wasn't an inkling of light because the power was off, and of course, we had no generator. Slowly we moved through the pitch dark, feeling our way through the master bedroom, and tried to find our way to the walk-in-closet. On the top rack, we laid hands on two kerosene oil lamps, a couple of flashlights, and finally some candles. We wrapped ourselves in multiple blankets and comforters. Between the oil lamps and the candles, the bedroom was lit up from one end of the room to the other, while adding a little warmth. Dallas and I called for my nephews and grandsons to come to the lower level. As with most teenagers, they were content in their own zone; consequently, we gave them lighting for the upstairs.

It was hazardous to be on the highways, and so we made do with what food we had in the refrigerator and cabinets. The electricity was out for days. In spite of the uncomfortable and awkwardness of the cold and no electricity, we hibernated under our covers. There were moments of stillness, and at other times we talked and talked and talked.

Our home was always kid-friendly, hilariously free, and funny. In addition to our three children, my two nephews (whom I raised) and the constant company of grandchildren. The children thought Dallas was so funny. I felt confident and happy with our relationship and that God gave me not only a gentleman with a good soul, but he had given me a mate with a unique name, Dallas.

Both of us were busy with ministry and school. We encouraged each other in our studies. As I've said before,

Dallas was excellent in lexicology, but a horrible speller. I needed toothpicks to keep my eyes open while literally sitting for hours helping him sound out and spell words. In return, he helped me with the definition and use of words I didn't understand.

Dallas was a blessing, in so many ways, to my children and me. It was easy for them to call him daddy. I grew to love him for his devotion, strength, faithfulness to the Lord, a man of few words, the way he treated me like a queen without all the royalties, and that he cared for my daughters. People have different perspectives and use a measurement by which each marriage partner is to give themselves. I was obliged that we were equal in our love, concern, and mutually made sure neither of us lacked. I grew to love Dallas for all the attributes that I could visibly see.

Brenda L. Moore | 48

Chapter 4

From Spring Showers to Tsunamis

One minute an ocean can be still and calm. The sky is bright and clear with a canvas of a beautiful formation of clouds. Then, without a moment's notice, the energy of the water creates turbulent waves; gloom and darkness cover the transparent sky because there is a severe storm approaching—a tsunami. A storm changes the elements of the heavens; a disturbance, intrusion, and inevitably destruction could occur. The extent of the damage remains a mystery until the storm hits. Life can be like this. Life can be calm and pleasant, and the next moment traumatic, thus leaving a ripple effect.

The storm in my marriage was enraged behavior. Dallas was aloof with bouts of silence, isolation, depression, deranged looks, lack of fortitude, excessive bitterness, anger, delusions, loss of interest in God, and his spiritual life, which all precipitated storms. His character changed to blaming, conflicting emotions, aggressiveness, hatefulness, diminishing relationships and, sad to say, Dallas burnt many bridges. The intensity of these storms created multiple problems that didn't deescalate.

For sure, there were more pleasant times in our family; however, when recollecting those instances, I couldn't seem to wrap my mind around them. As weeds choke out the beauty of a bed of flowers, in some instances, it was a symbol of our marriage. The bad became so overwhelming that it cast a deep shadow over the good times. Public outings, especially in restaurants, became repulsive. Vividly, I remember my husband's bulging eyes and panicky looks as he scanned the restaurant expecting that any moment something dangerous was about to happen.

In a place where a conversation should flow, instead, communication ceased. Dallas was preoccupied to the point he couldn't concentrate on me or why we were at the restaurant; consequently, we often ended up leaving shortly after we arrived. After many dinner plans flopped and we ended up going home, outings became such a disappointment I no longer desired to go out. I refused to go through the emotional upheaval. It only got worse.

Dallas would isolate himself, disappeared for days, weeks, and months at a time. He consistently wore dark shades, walked with his hands in his pockets, dragging slowly behind the children and me. He rambled with idol talk with himself and to the invisible. He went from a size 30-inch waist to 28 inches. His facial structure had a sunken look. He lay prostrate on the front porch of the College Chapel with students and staff having to step over his feeble body. In ninety-degree weather, Dallas wore a black leather jacket and cap with a pair of short black fingerless leather gloves and black army boots. His complexion was no longer a beautiful bronze color but of a deep grayish look of death. Instead of his warm, welcoming smile, he tightened his lips depicting arrogance and anger. He had become unapologetically territorial. He made a complete transformation from his spiritual life to nightclubbing, women, carousing, excessive drinking, and mingled with an entirely different type of associates.

Dallas's attire was still sharp but no longer represented a man of God, and he lived the life he once tried to distance himself from. His internal shadow took over the external shadow and no longer inseparable. His outward actions were clearly those of the pessimistic subconscious. Dallas was a changed man. I saw sides of him that were unfathomable.

When demented things happen, it leads one to reexamine. I had a flashback of Dallas and me exiting the back of the Louisville Veterans Hospital. Outside the entrance, set a trash can. Dallas stopped, took a bottle of pills from his pocket, and said, "I don't need these pills."

As he threw the bottle of pills into the trash container, I replied, "If you don't need the meds, don't take them." I am confident Dallas honestly felt it was the right thing to do because he had found a new relationship with Christ, positive people around him, and a woman he knew loved him for himself, so the newly found life would exclude or settle the brewing in his mind. Innocent and ignorant, I did not realize that agreeing with the disposal of those pills would be the beginning of many tsunamis in my marriage.

One evening following one of Dallas's disappearances, he came home. I sat on the arm of the couch while he sat in the recliner directly in front of me. The piercing look was a sign he was going to reveal something that was difficult for him. Then he hit me with the unthinkable, when he said, "I think I made a mistake getting married." The unexpected news was like getting a blow to my head, and it began to pound. Also, it appeared every nerve in my body was rattled. My anguished heart fluttered with conflicting emotions, and my stomach groaned with hurt. Needless to say, I didn't need more disappointment.

After he left the apartment, I pulled my body upstairs and stared out the bathroom window thinking, it's only been three months of marriage; surely, what this man threw in my lap couldn't be true. In habited by my thoughts, tears streamed down my cheeks. After the dreaded news, once again, he disappeared. Several days and nights passed, and he never came home. My brain was cluttered with questions. "What is wrong? Lord, who is this man? How can somebody change like this? Did I make a mistake? Devastatingly, I had to get out of the apartment in search of a serene environment in order to gain my composure and to think about where do I go from here?

In spite of my pain, I couldn't help feeling empathy for my husband. Maybe he is deeply grieved, and this was his way of releasing the children and me from the horrendous torment of his internal activities. One afternoon as I sat on the couch pondering what had taken place, a small voice said, *"The black bag, go upstairs and look in the black bag."* The voice continuously gnawed at my spirit. Physically not being in the mood to climb steps, I hesitantly obeyed and followed instructions. I went upstairs to the closet, and there sat the black leather case. Undoubtedly it was the Holy Spirit's doing. I stumbled on this black case several times and never felt the need to inquire about its content. Hurriedly, I proceeded to the bedroom and set the bag on my lap, not knowing what I was searching for. While fondling through photos of his Army Platoon and military friends, I became fixated on what looked like a certificate. It took a moment, as I carefully read, I realized the document I held in my hands were discharge papers from the United States Army.

Repeatedly, I read over the certificate because I was unaware of an honorable discharge. The emancipation from military duty was due to a mental impairment, *"chronic paranoid schizophrenia."* A heatwave came over my face. Although I didn't quite know the meaning of the medical term, common sense told me it was serious and severe enough for the Army to officially release him. The storm was unceasing. Horrified at finding the information, now I was scared and thought, "what was I supposed to do with the information?"

I found no need, nor was I comfortable enough to approach Dallas's family. After all, why wouldn't at least one of his family members let it be known their brother, son, uncle had a chronic illness? I didn't lose heart. In fact, God placed compassion in my spirit. Sometimes the best of us may think we know how to love, but it is not until the catastrophe of a storm comes in our life that love is tested. Slowly I lowered the black bag to the floor and placed the discharge papers on my chest, and asked God to please help me to help him. *"God is a very present help in the time of trouble." Psalms 46:1 (KJV). "The righteous cry and the Lord heareth and delivereth them out of their troubles." Psalms 34:17 (KJV*

After my plea, not only did God reveal to me the contents of the black bag, but there were also daytime TV talk shows, like the *Phil Donahue Show,* that provided information and resources on mental illness. Some of the discussions were defining schizophrenia and presenting a diagram of a schizophrenic's brain, theories for schizophrenia behaviors and medications, individuals and family testimonies, support groups, and much more. God answered my request by educating me through the media. I watched these same talk shows numerous times over the years, and never did I recall any form of this type of education. It was not coincidental, but divine.

My life was falling asunder. I conversed with myself and with God, "God, my heart is right. I know this relationship and marriage was from you. I was positive Dallas was my soul mate. How could I be so wrong?" Sincere as my thoughts were, the moments of grief and petitions to the Lord brought no relief. The storms kept coming. Problems escalated. Amazingly, why is it we women do not follow that first little voice. At any moment, we could look death in the face.

One evening Dallas asked me to go for a drive to his favorite hangout, Cox Park. Driving through the park, we passed by ball games and people picnicking. Dallas chose to drive to a secluded area of the park, a distance from where the action and activities took place where nothing going on was visible. In the wide-open space, all in view was land, rows of trees, and in between the trees were glimpses of the Ohio River. Dallas's face appeared solemn, but inwardly my gut feeling told me his *"internal shadow"* was doing its thing. It had not completely manifested itself, but something bizarre was about to happen. We walked in complete silence for a length of time. When I initiated a conversation, there was no response. Careful not to alarm him, I looked from my peripheral view and glanced quickly at his face. His frontal didn't look good. It was a little too late for me to follow my intuition.

The sun had gone down, the temperature had changed, and it was getting drafty and cool. You could see light rays from the lamp post throughout the park. Even then, there was no conversation and a blank look on my husband's face. Long before noticing his face, I had an overwhelming desire to leave. When I spoke of going home, Dallas's responded by placing his arm underneath my arm and proceeded walking me further into the park. Out in an open field, uncertain of my husband's thoughts or intentions, I knew the internal mind was working overtime. Now I am really scared.

Screaming was not an option. No one would ever hear me. I tried pulling away from him, and he pulled me by my clothes and set me down against a tree trunk. Then he gave the first sign of any communication since we entered the park. "Nah," he said. Time drug on and on. Night had settled. It was pitch dark, and I could neither see a peek of people, and vaguely I heard voices. It was my guess many people had left the park. Honestly, at this point, I questioned if I was going to return home. Confidently I knew Dallas would never hurt me. Nevertheless, I could not trust the "*internal shadow*" the unpredictability of schizophrenia. So, I did the one thing I learned to do well, pray, "God, please, help me."

After extremely long hours in Cox Park, we left the same way we came, which was in complete silence. I contributed our leaving to an answered prayer. I am so glad God is omnipresent. On the drive home, Dallas had a faraway look. Both of his hands gripped the wheel, and he looked straight ahead as if in a twilight zone. It was obvious he was not aware of the surroundings. My priority was to get home safely.

He drove into the driveway. Glad to be in a place of refuge, I wasted no time getting out of the car. Troubles strengthened me. I had a new assurance, my faith was elevated, and wisdom in such a time to call on the Lord. I thank God for delivering me.

More Secrets Tucked Away

Dallas's second cousin, Rhena, lived diagonally across from us. She came to visit and wanted to talk with me. I hadn't an inkling our conversation would be about my ex-husband, Edward, with whom she was contemplating marriage. So, she asked, "What can you tell me about Edward?" Reluctantly, I chose to do so briefly. I didn't want to appear negative because my marriage with him failed. However, for her sake, I revealed he was a domestic abuser. Her visit was one of those situations where she wanted to be informed yet had a made-up mind to pursue what she wanted in the first place. Consequently, our discussion revealed more secrets into my marriage with Dallas. Without directly telling me, Rhena informed me of a secret in the form of a question. "Did you know DD (nickname for Dallas) had a son?" I just sat there for a minute and stared. She must be mistaken. Rhena acted surprised that I didn't know. Incidentally, Rhena, and Edward did get married.

Rhena's news had my mind all over the place. "How could he have a child and keep it a secret? Are there more puzzle pieces missing? What other hidden secrets were there?" Occasionally during Dallas and my separations, I had the privilege of getting to know and taking care of my stepson, Lamar.

Prior to getting married, we vowed to get pregnant within one year. Even though the news that I was pregnant came at a crucial time, at least we followed through with one of our marriage plans. Anyhow the pregnancy came as a shock. My intrauterine device hadn't been removed, so how in the world could I be pregnant? Fortunately, my being pregnant turned out to be the "eye of the storm" in my life. After getting over the initial shock, the pregnancy brought tranquility for me.

One evening after being gone for some time, Dallas came strolling in the house. I shared with him the pregnancy with hopes he would embrace the news. I faced another disappointment. He stared at me with a blank countenance, turned his back, and all you could hear was army boots treading the wooden steps; never once did he look back. As Dallas stomped up the steps, he asked the most humiliating question. "Is it mine?" Not only had he insulted me, he crossed the line, insinuating I was disloyal. His sarcasm generated anger. I was too hurt to muster up the energy to lose my cool. I calmly said, "who else would it be?"

Speaking of unceasing storms, I went upstairs to prepare for bed when I heard a racket downstairs, which practically made me jump out of my skin. Without hesitation, I ran down the steps to see what was the matter? Like a stunt man, Dallas had put his entire body through my living room window. He prodded me upstairs and pushed me on the bed; he hit me in the eye, causing me to have a cornea infection. The pain was awful.

I laid in bed unconsciously, turning my wedding rings from side to side, feeling pity and disbelief for my situation. My perspective for wedding rings is they are tangible symbols of the commitment of love and marriage. Regardless of the value of my rings, which were rather costly, over $2725 to be exact, in retrospect of what our marriage had become, the rings had devalued; they had lost their beauty and were meaningless.

My pregnancy term passed quickly. Our son was born at 6:30 pm on August 24, 1983, at Saint Anthony

Hospital in Louisville, Kentucky. The second day of my hospital stay, in walked this man wearing a black leather jacket, cap pulled over his eyes, steel-toe boots, and dark shade glasses. Happy to see him, I asked, "Do you want to hold the baby?" Dallas looked at our baby, turned, and walked out of the hospital room. I wanted to curl up like an embryo and cry. You would think by then I'd be immune to the hurt.

Our son was given a fitting and Biblical name with a significant meaning of which I will talk about later. Without realizing the meaning of his name was a prediction of what was to come for our son's life, it correlated with issues which erected before he entered this world and a problematic future. He was rejected prior to birth and born into schizophrenia. My prayer and hope were that the mountains wouldn't become so high our son could not climb over them.

Chapter 5

Standing in the Shadows of Your Mate

The word shadow is defined as a reflected image, a dark figure cast on a surface by a body that is between the surface and light. It's a word that can generate a variety of perspectives. Some say it speaks of the *external and internal* shadow as being a mirage and indication of realness, and pretense. When I think of the meaning of shadow, it resembles a child's first observance of a dark silhouette below the feet. Have you ever observed and pitied a little child who, for the first time, recognizes their shadow and frantically screams, cries, and runs in different directions because the dark figure won't stop following them and just won't go away? A child is astounded by the movement of this dark resemblance of a person moving in every attempted direction. Running, coming to a stop, hopping, skipping, or whatever, the shadow remains a thorn in the child's spirit, making him/her feel victimized. I watched a child conclude that if he/she stopped, the shadow would not disappear; instead, it lingered and became more frightening. Inescapable.

A person's *external shadow* is visible and an exact resemblance or an authentic image. There is another shadow quite the opposite. It's invisible and has a hidden agenda. It can be demeaning and cause the external to evolve into a totally different character. This is called the *internal shadow.*

"When something is considered to be in the shadow, something has a bad influence to make another feel less enjoyable, attractive, and impressive. A person can keep you in their shadow by drawing attention to themselves by use of certain tactics, deceptions, and draw away attention onto them, attention they may see others give to you. Discouraging you from making great achievements/success…" Presley, Viola-June 30, 2013.

Ms. Presley is spot on. My husband was a replica of a shadow in my life. Like a force the attraction metal has to a magnet, wherever I went, I found myself involved with his issues in some way or another. Throughout my marriage and divorce, I felt like a child who could not escape their shadow.

"Shadow is an unconscious aspect of the personality which the conscious/ego does not identify. One tends to reject or remain ignorant of the least desirable of its personality. Unknown to the dark side of the personality/character, instinctive and irrational, psychological projections insulate and harm individuals by acting as a constant veil of illusion between the ego and the real world, becoming an enemy to oneself and refusal to acknowledge who we are."

"A battle of emotions, personal ideology viewing life as it is, what's happening in reality? The shadow personifies everything seen in others but refuses to

acknowledge about self. A tight passage, a narrow door,
whose painful constriction, will not allow anyone to go
down to that "deep well." The person cannot see self but
can plainly see egotism, mental laziness, unreal fantasies,
schemes/plots, carelessness, cowardice, inordinate love of
money and possessions…The black shadow everyone
carries with him, the inferior aspect of the personality."
Carl G. Jung

My spirit resonates with Jung's ideology, especially being accused of negative behaviors. What was so appalling was the accusations made were the exact characteristics of Dallas's personality depending on the day, anger and frustrations festered. When this happened, I felt pressed to scream and yell, "Are you out of your mind? That's you!" I was not alone. Family, friends, and church family grew tired and disturbed with the accusations as well. Dallas saw the wrong in the church, friends, family, and the world, yet he found it difficult to go in that "dark well" of his inner self. The internal mind will often oppose and overwhelm a person's external. When this happens, the outward man/woman portrays internal feelings. His confused and chaotic subconscious mind, paralyzed by indecisiveness, fears, and distorted thinking produces unbridled and intemperate actions.

"One who is possessed by the inner shadow is always standing in his own light and falling into his own traps... lives below his own level." Carl G. Jung

My husband became preoccupied, consumed with the problems and behaviors of people, so he became a pantomath. He had the answer to their problems. Avoidance became a defense mechanism. Observation of his tactics and manipulative ways opened my eyes to the fact that folks need a disguise or something to hide behind and to absorb themselves in the crisis of others in order to divert attention from their personal issues, phobias, and subconscious.

I had acquaintances who shared their desire to choose a profession such as (counselor, psychiatrist). Knowing the circumstances of each individual while intensely listening, my thoughts were, *it's only to camouflage the real you.* In several instances, Dallas acknowledged he would be good in the field of psychology. Without a doubt, it was clear as to why he wanted to pursue this profession. Thank God his thoughts didn't become a reality. I don't know who would have suffered more, him, patients, or both. Jesus spoke of reflecting the weakness of others.

Sporadically, our life together became intense, complicated, and problematic. Some of our most wonderful lines of communication were discussions connecting life with the scriptures; then, it too became confrontational. Disagreements led to arguments. No longer did he care to make an application to self, to our relationship, and our family. Yes, I know, they say, "It takes two to argue." I was sick and tired of pessimism, skepticism, and lack of ownership of his mistakes, etc. Escape from communication before the discussion could formulate usually began with, *"Why you always wanna argue?"*

It was years before my husband could acknowledge and somewhat <u>handle</u> the downside of him, which was robbing him of a sound mind of the person he could be, relationships, and family. *"The heart is deceitful above all things, and desperately wicked; who can know it?" Jeremiah 17:9 (NKJV)" "O wretched man that I am, who will deliver me from this body of death? I thank God through Jesus Christ our Lord." Romans 7:24-25 (NKJV)*

Shadow of Emotions

Are you real, or just a figment of my imagination, a pretense?

Sunup and sundown; a fit of rage, each time darker than the first

Extreme tranquility, which I want to stay, appear then

disappear and reappear

Daily uncertainties of which will materialize

Lost in perplexity

Shadow, I can't figure you out.

At the beginning of this chapter, I alluded to there being different perspectives of the shadow. A shadow can also be a problem that one finds extremely difficult to overcome. I don't know what your shadow is. It could be the death of a child, spouse, parent, addiction, divorce, financial problems, physical sickness, constant bad decisions, significant other, or maybe like mine, mental illness, whatever the case may be, *"nothing is impossible with God."*

Chapter 6

The Walls Behind Closed Doors

Walls are structured for adaptable reasons. They divide or conquer, protect, shield, serve as a barrier, and more. Regardless of what takes place outside your shelter, it's good to know refuge can be taken behind the walls of your home. Behind those walls, there should be a covering of peace, safety, and stability from evils lurking outside.

Over the years, the conditions of my life with Dallas made me feel as though the walls were closing in on me every time I went to our home. More often than not, I looked forward to tranquility outside the circumference of our home. The walls of my home were unbalanced, troubling, and full of unpredictability. Like a war zone, at times coming home was like stepping on a land mine. I battled with my husband's illness while trying to keep Satan from consuming me. In fact, if my walls could talk, they would speak a different version of the external me which people saw. My walls would expose the pain behind my eyes and reveal inwardly I was a shattered vase. Although disheartened, God directed me to reach within myself to protract a genuine smile and lead me in my daily purpose. He urged me to place my weak hands in His strong hands.

The Book of Ecclesiastes speaks of fish suddenly caught in a cruel net. My husband and I were a couple trapped in unexpected evil. I became aware of what it meant to wrestle against powers and wickedness in high places. There were nights I laid my head on Dallas's chest as water streamed from my eyes while I poured out my heart in prayer. "God, please, take it away this illness. God, if you are testing me, I have shown you I will continue to be loyal. I am not going anywhere. I am here to stay no matter what." The more I prayed, the worst things got. Numerous times I made this request of God, thoughts of the

Apostle Paul came to mind. He prayed three times for the Lord to take away a weakness of the flesh, *and* God replied, *"My grace is sufficient."*

God, in His infinite wisdom, won't always extract the problem but will provide the spiritual armor necessary to hold us during life's challenges. There were nights, gentle moments calmed the demons behind my walls. During bedtime, as my husband slept, he had a habit of holding me in his arms. A time I felt safe. Unfortunately, this particular night was like none other. While in the embrace of my husband's arms, I was awakened by strange sounds or voices similar toa surgical voice box. It was bewildering. While my husband's face lay on my neck, I could not feel any lip movement, and neither could I feel the warmth of his breath. Strangely, the weird voices appeared to come from within. It was as if someone put a defective tape recorder inside him, he had an electrolarynx device, or someone was talking through him. I couldn't move. The more tuned in I was, the more boisterous the voices became. Although the chattering language was muzzling, some words were loud and clear. The voices bellowed derogatory remarks, of which I care not to repeat, spurts of profanity, and mockery regarding the Church.

Wrapped in his arms took on an entirely new turn. Actually, I felt more like I was in a straitjacket. I was scared to open my eyes and too terrified of what I might see. However, I managed to quickly open and shut my eyes to the darkness of our bedroom, while seriously thinking should I call out my husband's name. Should I try moving from his grip? A familiar voice, the Holy Spirit, whispered over and over, "*Lay there. Be still.* I obeyed. Silently and repetitively, I spoke the name of Jesus. The next time I opened my eyes, it was daylight.

My husband's body frame was frail; he was down to a 28" or 29" waistline. His face was sunken, which overly emphasized his cheekbones. With slanted eyes and a grayish complexion, Dallas looked like death itself. He had gone months without medication and was too far gone to be convinced he needed help. At this point, mental illness consumed my husband.

Weeks later, we had a visitor, Sister Janet Wilson, a true warrior whom I had the privilege to be a mentee. She was a strong, tenacious woman, Bible Teacher, Evangelist, Missionary, and mighty in faith. Most important to me was her strong influence in my life as we frequently worshiped and prayed together. We worked in Vacation Bible Study, traveled to women's retreats, and she also gave me my first experience doing mission work and teaching in Haiti.

Due to the nature of her work, Sister Wilson was no stranger to problems and understood troubled walls. She loved my husband, was aware of his mental state and recognized his untapped potential. Her visit was not a casual one. My husband sat on the couch while Sister Wilson and I set in individual chairs directly in front of him. She took control of the visit and was intense in her persuasion, using skill and wisdom to gently press him to reach out for help. While Sister Wilson was talking, I became distracted by my husband's pupils. His eyes were abnormally dilated, and directly in the middle of his pupils were glaring lights in the shape of a small twinkling star yet consistently jumping up and down. It was a scary look, and I was solely fixated on it. My thoughts were, "Oh my God. Are these demons?" I witnessed first-hand the invasion of wickedness occupying space in the body of one of God's children. Sister Wilson was still heightened and compelling Dallas to get help at the Veterans Hospital. My eyes still locked on my husband, I pondered if Sister Wilson observed what I saw. She ended the one-sided conversation with a passionate prayer. It was no doubt Dallas's commitment to silence wasn't derived from spite. For him, it could have been for several reasons because he had the highest regard for Sister Wilson's advice. He lifted his frail body from the sofa and walked out the door. As soon as the door slammed shut behind my husband, Sister Wilson could hardly contain herself as she quickly turned toward me, elbowed me in the side, and shouted, "Did you see them? Did you see those demons?" Her spirit aroused me that much more. I studied scriptures about demonic spirits possessing and residing in humans. My ears heard, my eyes saw, and I know demons are real, and they do exist. Thank you, Jesus, on that day they left out the door with my husband.

Those moments with Sister Wilson and my husband taught me some unforgettable lessons. First, it is dangerous to omit God and the spiritual from our life. Omitting worship and avoiding people of faith leaves space for Satan and other demons to occupy our bodies and take control. *"Then goeth he, and taketh with himself seven other spirits more wicked than himself, and they enter in and dwell*

there: and the last state of that man is worse than the first."
Matthew 12:45 (KJV)

Second, demonic spirits can only control the body
through ignorance and refusal to allow God's Word to
penetrate the mind and heart. Denial of truth intensifies the
"internal shadows," which keep the mind captive. It
became easier for Dallas to choose wrong and harder to do
what was right. His once unyielding faith was fading daily.
What was worse, Satan used my husband's thorn to destroy
his relationship with God, family, and others. Despicable
actions monopolized his days and nights. Hurting others
became a sense of self- gratification for his anger and
bitterness. *"Neither give place to the devil." Ephesians
4:27 (KJV)*

Erratic behaviors behind our walls continued.
Following a long day at school, I came home and went
upstairs to find every stitch of clothing in my closet was
shredded to pieces except for two dresses that were barely

hanging on hangers. My mouth dropped with unbelief. What possessed him to cut up my clothes. Every day I had a phobia of stepping on landmines of uncertainty and anticipation of the unexpected behind our walls.

My husband's presence in our home was sporadic. What was questionable was when he did show up, would his character and presence be of good or some evil? The one thing that was sure I knew God resided in the midst of my troubling walls.

"Even though I walk through the darkest valley, I will fear no evil, for you are with me, your rod and your staff, they comfort me…" Psalms 23:4 (NIV)

Stay Prayed Up

Prayer is a privilege given to all believers who claim Jesus as the Son of God. It is open communication with the Father, Son, and the Holy Spirit. No matter how strong you think your walls are, at one time or another, the foundation can become weak, shaken, and sometimes may collapse. It is imperative to stay connected with God because He is the only one who will be able to give you the strength to maintain beneath the weight and to eradicate strongholds. Prayer entails six components:

➢ Acknowledging God

➢ Make your request, weakness, the intent of our heart known unto God

➢ Expectations and listening for a response from God

➢ Knowing He is faithful, keeps His promises and cannot lie. No matter how long, wait on God

➢ Accepting God's answer: Yes, No, Not Now, or Wait

➢ You and God have a part in the ordeal, do your part

After this manner therefore pray ye: Our Father which art in heaven, Hallowed be thy name…" Matthew 6:9-13 (KJV)

Meditate, pray, and allow time for God to speak to your spirit. Read the Word for the Holy Spirit doesn't work apart from the scriptures. Together, they provide and equip us with wisdom, direction, and instruction in <u>all</u> things.

"Be careful for nothing; but in everything by prayer and supplication with thanksgiving let your requests be made known unto God." Philippians 4:6 (KJV) "All scripture is is given by inspiration of God, and is profitable for doctrine, for reproof, for correction, for instruction in righteousness:" II Timothy 3:16 (KJV)

God's Timing

Have you ever asked God for something then when He delivers it, you had forgotten you requested it of Him? God is faithful, even in our unfaithfulness. God listens and responds to our request, according to His divine will and time. Prayer is growing in intimacy with God. He is Omnipresent. On days we feel God is silent and distant, He is working behind the scenes for our good and to fulfill His purpose in our lives. When I think of God, I realize He doesn't waste time as man often does. God is Sovereign, (*Supreme Ruler and Lord*), over humanity.

The providence of God and His hand is in and over all things pertaining to this world.   In time, nature does exactly what it is supposed to do. How much more is this true in terms of humanity. We are created in the Master's image. God takes the good and bad to work in an individual's daily life for a greater good. He is fitting us for eternity. *"And we know that all things work together for good to them that love God..." Romans 8:28 (KJV)*

Advantages and Power of Collective Prayers

Pay close attention to this excerpted article by Peter Cructchley, *"The Berlin wall was a structure of concrete and barbed wire between east and West Berlin. The wall had two symbols: Communist oppression: Symbol, a suppression of human rights. For 30 years, the Berlin Wall defined the cold war, separated families, and kept people from jobs and the opportunity in the west.   An accumulation of years, the Saint Nikolai Church in East*

Germany, the city, along with children, Christians, and

Atheists, gathered and organized prayer meetings. The

peace prayers spread. The article posed a question as to

whether or not prayer had something to do with the Berlin

walls coming down.

    "October 9, 1989 (Leipzig), one month before the

fall of the Berlin Wall, Pastor Christian Fuhrer organized

an impromptu peace rally (protest/prayer)*, of*

approximately 70,000-300,000 people. Streets were

barricaded, death threats were made, armed Police

Officers were in hopes of putting people off, but it had the

opposite effect. The Protestors walked slowly around the

city. The crowd ignored the threats, and they weren't

attacked."

    "November 9, 1989, the Berlin Wall came down.

...Unification and prayers continued even after the fall. The

Bible taught them the power of prayer and peaceful protest.

Pastor Fuhrer exclaimed, "The church has to do it; to this
day, the Church still has to do it." PC "Did a Prayer
Meeting Bring Down the Berlin Wall?" Cructchley, Peter,
Nov. 2013: Berlin_wall.coldwar.history.com

Reading this article caused me to revisit the history
of my ancestors, who were known for community and
collective prayer as they pressed through the hardships and
vulnerability during slavery. Dr. Martin Luther King Jr., a
pastor and civil rights movement leader, understood
collectively joining forces in peaceful protesting and
prayers. In Joshua 6:1-27, God gave Joshua marching
orders around the city of Jericho which resulted in a
victory. In summary, the city of Jericho was the Israelite's
first hurdle on the way to the promised land, Canaan. The
people encountered the wall built around Jericho angled 35
ft. upward, joining massive stone walls towering higher.
Specific instructions were given to Joshua, the new leader
of the Israelites. Instructions were for Israel to march

around silently for six days, and on the seventh day, Joshua and the people were to march around seven times. The priests were to blow their trumpets, and they let out a shout. There had to be continuity and extensive prayer taking place. When Joshua obeyed God's instructions, the walls of Jericho collapsed.

Prayer teaches:

➢ God is not confined by any man or man-made object.

➢ God is not controlled by time but is in control of time.

➢ God always has a plan (A) and does not need a plan (B).

➢ God's plan and instructions are direct and specific.

➢ God's plan comes with warnings and judgment.

➢ God's plan doesn't always make sense.

➢ God's plan is absolute. It cannot be altered. It cannot be deterred.

➢ Christians have to get on board with the plan of God.

➢ God's plan is authoritative and overrides man's plans.

"For my thoughts are not your thoughts, neither are your ways my ways, saith the LORD." Isaiah 55:8-9 (KJV)

"Commit thy works unto the LORD, and thy thoughts shall be established."Proverbs16:3 (KJV)

Prayers should never be considered insignificant, something we just do on the spare of the moment or when it fits into our schedules. Problems will occur, which call for collaborative prayers and belief that our Heavenly Father is bigger than any problem we inhabit. Forfeiting prayer leads to spiritual weakness, vulnerability, a lack of faith, and self-reliance versus God's reliance.

"The effectual fervent prayer of a righteous man availeth much." James 5:16 (KJV). *"Pray without ceasing."* I Thessalonians 5:17 (KJV)

The Devil is cynical and suggests thoughts that deter us from individual and collective prayers. We must be aware of his tactics, and here are a few:

- He wants us to think we can remain fleshly while, at the same time, think our prayers are reaching God. *"And I, brethren, could not speak to you as to spiritual people but as to carnal, as to babes in Christ. I fed you with milk and not with solid food; for until now you were not able to receive it, and even now you are still not able; for you are still carnal." I Corinthians 3:1-3 (NKJV)*

- We've done too much wrong or something so bad, God won't hear our prayers.

- At the mere sign of trouble-we go directly to social media, phones, Facebook, Twitter, Instagram, blogs, Chit Chat, texting, and email, to air and exploit personal problems and our business to the public, friends, and family or whoever will listen, all before we consult God.

  "Call to me and I will answer you…" Jeremiah 33:3 (NKJV) "Let us therefore come boldly unto the throne

of grace, that we may obtain mercy, and find grace to help in time of need." Hebrew 4:16 (KJV)

At times, immediate and church family can provide inspiration and relevant scriptures. What I am alluding to is the time wasted when we don't choose to consult God first. People can't solve our problems. In their frailty, they too need God; therefore, how can they help you solve yours? *"God is our refuge and strength, a very present help in trouble." Psalms 46:1 (KJV)*

Behind the walls of my home, nothing was hidden from the Almighty who never *"sleeps nor slumbers."* God kept me from harm. What is behind your walls may not be the same as mine. Believe in this one thing. When God decides it's Demo Day, He will tear down walls.

➢ Walls of hate and racism

➢ Walls of insecurities

➢ Walls of police brutality

➢ Walls of racial profiling

- Walls of depression and suicides

- Walls of addictions

- Walls of sexual promiscuity and sex trafficking

- Walls of communism

- Walls of political corruptness

- Walls of poverty

- Walls of gun violence and crimes on humanity

- Walls of corrupt social media

- Walls of terrorism and war

- Walls of false religions

- Walls of incarceration

"For in the time of trouble he shall hide me in his pavilion: in the secret of his tabernacle shall he hide me." *Psalms 27:5 (KJV).* Jeremiah 38:1-28 gives an example of walls encountered by the Prophet Jeremiah when he was lowered by ropes down into a 30 ft. cistern because he spoke judgment from God to the people. Ebed-Melech, a Eunuch approached the King on behalf of Jeremiah… The

King ordered his release. I am sure Jeremiah became somewhat phobic and saw no form of escape from sunken mud and clay walls which surrounded him. Jeremiah could have overwhelmed himself by making the walls of the pot his focal point. I could imagine Jeremiah found himself on his knees with no alternative but to look up. It was then he saw a beam of light from the opening in the cistern, a ray of hope.

All God requires is for us to see a glimpse of Him and to have a mustard seed size faith. Like the prophet, Jeremiah, there will be days people will cause you to feel as if you are sunk in the mud, closed in, and not know which way to turn. No matter what the demographics are, the circumstances, or the mass crowds, look toward Heaven and don't lose consciousness of God. *"Be not afraid of their faces: for I am with thee to deliver thee, saith the LORD." Jeremiah 1:8 (KJV)*

Why the Emphasis on Prayer?

Prayer does not mean being equipped with elaborate words and eloquent speech. We don't always have the words to speak to God. The Apostle Paul said, *"When I am weak, then I am made strong." Prayer* is simply being humble, honest, and direct before God. The Bible tells us, *"nothing is too hard for God."*

Had it not been for prayer, my walls would have closed in on me. It was through prayer the Lord showed me Satan was working through my husband's illness to destroy me and that my circumstances may or may not change. So, God directed my attention toward changing me so that I could endure. My faith didn't fail me, nor did I lose sight of to whom I belong. I still had a purpose and spiritual standards to uphold.

"Not by might, nor by power, but by my spirit, saith the LORD of hosts." Zechariah 4:6 (KJV)

Chapter 7

A Good Run is Better Than a Bad Stand

I contacted a close friend who lived in Danville, Illinois, and asked if she could accommodate the children and me. I needed to put space between me and my walls, to seek a new atmosphere to clear my mind—a getaway. Quietly, I left Louisville traveling to Danville. The city reminded me of the cozy small town of Mayberry, a community depicted in the 60's TV sitcom "The Andy Griffin Show." Promptly at noon, buses from the city's transit service, known as *"The Run Around,"* lined up in front of the main drug store waiting for the passengers. One never had to worry about being stranded because the drivers knew the passenger's faces, names, and times they boarded the bus and waited patiently. Seemly it only took ten to fifteen minutes to arrive at a grocery store or restaurant. Danville certainly had a much slower pace than Louisville.

I had no intention of moving from Louisville, but I felt I could get used to the small town and its friendly environment. At times, my heart yearned for Dallas and back home, although I had to admit there was a calmness in his absence. In spite of what I was tunneling through, I had a responsibility to keep my children happy. I quickly adapted to my new peaceful space and delighted in the fact there was not an incline of violence or distractions of any kind.

I attended the Collett Street Church of Christ and became involved. My days and weeks were full serving in areas of leadership for the women's ministry, teaching a Bible class, and occasionally on Sunday mornings, I led the congregational singing. The kindness of the sisters and brothers at Collett Street Church made my stay pleasant. In addition to becoming involved in church work, it was my endeavor to pick up where I left off at the College of the Scriptures in Louisville and continue in my major, Christian Education. My desire was to become a Bible teacher for a Christian School or Academy. As I continued to tour the city, I became acquainted with the lifestyle, checked out the schools for myself and the children, and looked for organizations and job opportunities. I soon recognized the opportunities in these areas were slim. The town had one major drug store, a county market, and a limited number of fast food and sit-down restaurants.

Danville had one college, Danville Community College, one elementary and one high school, which was Danville Elementary and Danville High. It was then I concluded it would be difficult for my children to expand their knowledge/career in such an undeveloped town. Job opportunities were rare unless you knew someone already established. Regrettably, there were no Christian schools, and if I was going to reside in Danville, I might have to consider a new major or career. It was a big disappointment because Christian teaching was imperative for me, and definitely one gift I loved and possessed. I resorted to changing my major to Interdisciplinary Early Childhood Education. The lesson I learned was, life will alter your plans.

Starting Over

I applied for a grant and enrolled in Danville Community College. Immediately I was hired as a Counselor/Social/Program Director for minority students. My work experience and responsibilities were the same as working for the College of the Scriptures in Louisville but on a larger scale. I assisted out-of-town students on educational trips, preparation, and soliciting professional educators as speakers for workshops, planned social programs for the college, and directed students to tutorial programs and financing on campus. More opportunities became accessible.

After a while, my living arrangements weren't working so well. The children and I stayed with an older sister in our church until I was financially stable. I was fortunate to have rented a townhouse owned by one of the sisters at the church. It was such a good feeling to have a place to set my own rules, boundaries, and freedom for my children to play. Also, living on the second floor made me feel secure from the shadows of Louisville.

The apartment consists of a large master bedroom, bathroom, a living room, and a large kitchen. I loved it with the exception of one big problem. One night I turned on the kitchen light and got the surprise of my life, the brown paneled walls were covered with roaches running wild. I thought I was going to be sick. Strangely enough, the pest appeared to be confined to the kitchen because I never saw any roaches in our bedroom or the living room, which made it tolerable until the weekend. The following Sunday I talked with the owners about an exterminator.

I wanted to make my children's move as smooth as possible, so we continued routines they were accustomed to as a family in Louisville and also made new memories. Since we moved quickly, I wanted my children to relax and hopefully it would ease their loneliness. Some major holidays were coming up, for example, Halloween. This was not a favorable holiday for me, but being a teacher and a parent, I knew how to make this day fun. In Louisville, people had begun to set up pranks for kids, like putting razor blades in apples etc., to the point, hospitals requested parents bring their children's candy bags to the hospital to be x-rayed for anything harmful. Personally, I was uncomfortable taking my children door to door since we were new to the city. So, I put my imagination to work by creating my own inside Halloween fun. I prepared, finger sandwiches, chips, large bowls of candy and bubble gum, homemade caramel popcorn balls, candy apples, sodas, and since it was cold, we had hot chocolate. We played musical chairs and I set up an indoor musical scavenger hunt using candy and gifts for prizes. We had a blast.

On Thanksgiving we had family dinner with the church, which helped us become more familiar with our church family and friends. Christmas was a big time for us at our house. The family gathered around a table centered in the middle of the Eagle Family Room. We began with one person at a time, beginning with the youngest child to the adults. Each person would place their gift on the table in front of another person and we all watched until that person opened all their gifts, and then we would go to the next age. Following gift opening we assembled upstairs in the living room and dining room for Christmas dinner.

In Danville, tradition would have to be broken and so I began with Christmas Eve fun. I found the same enjoyment baking cookies from scratch and watching Tameka, Knijel, and little Aaron lick the cookie mix bowl. I enjoyed watching them put their choice of food coloring in the cream cheese icing and seeing the outcome of each one's creative sprinkler designs.

My children and I shared the large master bedroom. Each of the girls had a window where I hung frilly baby blue sheer/ruffled curtains. The girls had twin beds with gold headboards and each one had a beautiful matching blue bedspread and pillow shams. The blue curtains and matching spreads gave the room a pretty glow. A place on the opposite side of the room was created just for their toys. Aaron had his bed as well, but he was content with stashing his toys. Making my children happy was a priority and the highlight of my life. *"Either you run the day, or the day runs you." Jim Rohn*

Although I hadn't decided to make Danville my home, it had begun to feel like it. Perhaps it could've been the fact my mother taught me that wherever I live, I should make it my home. Nonetheless, the past has a way of tracking you. I began dealing with walls of unease, fearfulness, and tension.   After two months, at night after tucking my babies in bed, I headed straight for my side of the room and what I believed was going to be a restful night of sleep on the couch. Instead many nights I found myself having a queasy stomach from jumping at annoying sounds and the opening and shutting of the downstairs entrance door.

What struck me as being footsteps approaching my apartment door was really a figment of my imagination. Who else could be coming up my steps? Wondering how Dallas could have found my address so quickly, I told myself the noises were just the settling of the walls in an old building. Some nights I laid there, wide eyed and focused on the hallway light peering beneath the crack underneath my apartment door, looking for a figure of a human shadow.   The worst was my staring at the ceiling for hours, looking around the room; not understanding why my tired body refused to fall asleep.

The longevity of sleeplessness took its toll. I lay there at night anxious for the sunlight to peak between the blue curtains, just so I would no longer lie in torment. When my body should have rested it was grossly fatigued. "Why couldn't I go to sleep? What was wrong with me?" Is this what insomnia feels like? What I was going through was a replay of the horrific experiences that plagued me in Louisville. Quite the contrary, when morning came, I experienced God's new mercies. God makes a way to escape. Sleepless nights and physical tiredness gave way to resilience, perseverance, and endurance. God enabled me to rise and go about my daily routine. *"It is the Lord's mercies that we are not consumed…They are new every morning: great is thy faithfulness." Lamentations 3:22-23 (KJV)* Psalms 12:1-4 tells me God's mercy never runs out.

Chapter 8

Learn to Listen When God Speaks.

Praying is one thing, listening for God's voice and getting an understanding doesn't always come easy. Prayer is a vital entity of communication and connection with God. It is of greater importance to be aware of three integral parts to communication with God: *speaking*, *meditation*, and *listening*. Knowing <u>when</u> the Lord is <u>speaking</u> to you takes much discernment.

Speaking is simply having an intimate talk with God. Speaking on our deepest thoughts, sharing our needs, wants, admiration, praise, and thanksgiving among many other concerns, depending on the individual.

Meditation is taking the time to ponder, read scriptures pertaining to your needs and requests as you wait and listen for God's voice. It's a time to slow down and settle yourself. Meditation allows you to perceive every situation, then you can see your request doesn't always require an immediate answer nor is it necessary to readily go into action. When we are hasty in decision making, we get into trouble and when it doesn't work out, we blame God. Meditation is getting an understanding of what God is trying to say, and how he is guiding and directing in response to your need. It prepares you to accept what God says and allows, even if there is a delay in His response. You understand that God doesn't forget, put us off, and keep us in limbo. You understand that He always answers on time. Last, meditation is not being satisfied with telling yourself you've prayed or consulted God while knowing you are totally not interested in God's answer more than you are taking matters in your own hand.

Listening is anticipation and expectancy that what you ask of God, He will answer, and He will respond to our request and need according to His will.

Shortly after my children and I moved and were settled in our new place in Danville, on a Monday afternoon, there was a knock at the door. It was a sister from the church who came to deliver a message, and she didn't waste any time. "Brenda—Sister Wilson from Louisville called, and says it's urgent. She needs you to return the call right away." My adrenaline was going, and I jumped to the conclusion it was bad news. Although I was hoping no one was sick, I also knew that if Sister Wilson sent a message of this sort, it was serious.

I didn't own a phone, and the nearest phone booth was quite a distance. I strolled across the baseball field, anticipating the conversation. I dialed her number, and Sister Wilson picked up quickly as if she were waiting by the phone or automatically knew it was me calling. "Hi, darling." Following her greeting, in a sweet candid tone, she explained, "Family needs to be together, and Dallas had changed." I summed up our entire conversation with Sister

Wilson's case and point. Why didn't I return to Louisville and give it a try? She did most of the talking as I listened. My reply to her request was I would think about it.

The sky was cloudy and looked as though it would rain as I started the long walk back across the baseball field. When I got midway across the field, it began to rain heavily. Uneasy and confused, my face was a mixture of tears and rain. However, I was not affected much by the downpour because my mind was drenched with thoughts of my inner spirit shouting, *it's not a good idea.*

I walked and talked and question God. "God, I am scared. I don't know. Am I supposed to return to Louisville? I don't want to go back, but if You want, I will. If I do, God please, You have to protect me. God, if I don't go back and it was Your will…"

The will to alleviate fear from being disobedient to God and follow what was right was something that overshadowed me. The truth of the matter is, I didn't give myself more time to speak to God to meditate and listen. I wasn't wise enough to understand it wasn't a matter of life or death for me to go back to Louisville right away. There were many things I didn't register nor considered. That's when the Holy Spirit said, *"It's not a good idea."* God was saying no, or it's not time. My intentions weren't to place Sister Wilson on a pedestal, but I respected her advice. Given her faith and spirit, surely, she must have heard from God.

I also have been a little bit of a risk-taker if it meant doing something right and beneficial. Right away, I planned for the girls to remain in Danville. Aaron and I returned to Louisville on a Greyhound Bus. My heart was right, and I conversed back and forth with God. But was I really listening? My second day back in Louisville, I sat at the kitchen table in my apartment, of which I had not yet given up, just a few feet away from the sliding doors. On that day, things quickly turned for the worse, and it then became clear. Instantaneously, before my eyes could take in what happened, I heard glass shatter. Pieces of glass fell inside and outside the door frame. The next thing I saw was Dallas stepping through the metal frame of the glass door. Oh, my God. I thought this couldn't be happening again. Previously, we had lived in an apartment, and I witnessed Dallas put his entire body through the front window; this instance was like watching a Jet Li movie as Dallas used his Black-Kwan-Doe skills to kick in the glass door. After I actualized what took place, my instincts were to run. Feeling his touch slightly grab me by the arm, I was able to break loose and ran out my front door toward the office adjacent to my apartment.

Dallas caught up, threw me to the ground, and began kicking me over and over. The more I struggled to get up, the more he kicked. Effortlessly between using my hands and elbows to dodge the kicks, I managed to look up to the faces of a shouting crowd hovering over me. Never would I'd ever believed he could be this violent, not the man I grew to love. There could be no denying; Dallas was out of control. Undoubtedly, my sister, Anna, who lived up the street had gotten wind of the commotion and had pushed through to the front of the crowd because the next figure I saw was her face leaning over me. I remember her holding a broom handle, repeatedly striking Dallas and, at the same time, yelling, "Run Brenda. Run Brenda. Run." Exhausted and gasping for breath, I managed to get to my feet and ran back into the apartment.

I started toward the broken patio door to take a peek to see if Dallas had left the premises. With all that had abruptly taken place, I hadn't realized our baby had come downstairs and gone outside. I saw Dallas putting our son, Aaron, in the car. Knowing his psychotic state, I screamed his name and pleaded for him to leave Aaron. My fingers trembled as I dialed his phone with panicking thoughts of Aaron being hurt. My calls were going straight to voicemail. More anguish set in knowing Aaron had become a victim.

There was no alternative but to dial 911 for the police. It took a minute for the officers to arrive. Following my explanation of the incident, one officer nonchalantly explained Aaron was Dallas's son, and since no custody order was in place, nothing could be done. Tragically, in the '80s, domestic abuse was not taken seriously, and not much empathy was shown toward women victims. In my opinion, the maltreater had more rights.

The following day I received a call from the secretary of the College of the Scriptures. She informed me Dallas had brought our baby to her home, and she convinced him to take Aaron home. When Dallas arrived, there were no spoken words between us, and that was fine with me. Once I reached out to Aaron and had him safe in my arms, I clung to him and he to me. I knew he could feel the tension. My instincts were right; due to the aggressiveness, Dallas used to put Aaron in the car; somehow, his face must have hit something because his eye was swollen almost closed. Aaron was the sweetest and meekest little boy, which made it twice as hard for me to see him hurt.

I went upstairs and stood at the bathroom window, only this time, I was not looking for Dallas to come home. Deep mourning, humiliation, and disappointment accompanied a flow of tears. A familiar voice spoke, *"move."* Before the thought faded, my sister Anna walked beside me and confirmed the Holy Spirit's leading as she said softly, "Brenda, you need to move." Sniffling from the tears, I replied, "I know." I will always be grateful for her being there for me.

Anyway, it was a clear affirmation that I shouldn't have returned to Louisville, and I hadn't listened to God. From this calamity, I found further clarity. No longer was

Danville, Illinois, to be a temporary getaway. It was to be my permanent home, at least for the present. As a result of my studying, I was wise enough to remember God could take a situation gone wrong and work it out for good.

Leaving Louisville would take careful strategic planning. Most likely, on a Sunday morning, Dallas would be at worship, and his expectations would be to see us there. I contacted one of the church members who owned a truck. With as little details as possible, I briefly explained that as early as possible on Sunday morning, I needed my bare essentials loaded on the truck. I knew Dallas's unpredictability, for it wasn't out of the norm for him to show up on Saturday in the middle of the night, knowing I was still in town. However, thank God, he didn't, and needless to say, I didn't get much sleep from packing and wishing for daylight. On Sunday morning, all went as planned. By 11 a.m. the truck was loaded, and around 2:30

p.m. Sunday afternoon, my children and I became residents in Danville, Illinois.

A number of lessons were learned from that horrific experience. Be quick to process and slow to react. I reiterate. Give yourself space to consult with God and ask Him what it is that He's telling you. Then give Him time to answer. The longevity of a person's church life, educational status, or theological knowledge is no indication that person has the spiritual capability to understand and know the will of God for you. And I realized I had an obligation to God and to myself to learn to differentiate between the voice of God and people's personal perceptions.

Although it may be of innocence and with good intentions, Christians have a habit of interfering in the spiritual lives of others while thinking they've been blessed with a "high calling" to reveal God's will for another's plight. The danger of this frame of thinking is these people act as though God substantiates their personal beliefs and conclusions when what should be done is to extend words of encouragement, pray with them, and direct the individual's mind back to God for an answer. Trouble prevails when trusting self-wisdom to speak for God.

The Bible speaks of occurrences when people took matters in their hands to interfere in the plan(s) of God. "During Biblical times, child-barren women were looked down upon. Sara, Abram's wife, was one of those women, and she was also past the child-bearing age. Sara listened outside the tent as God told her husband, Abram, that within one year, she would have a child. Sara laughed in denial. Persistent and impatience prompted Sara to request of Abram to have intercourse with her handmaid, Hagar. As a result, Hagar became pregnant with a son named Ishmael. Sara's spirit became jealous and spiteful, so she sent Hagar and the child away. God was displeased and didn't alter His plans based on Sara's emotions. Based on past demonstrations, Sara failed to remember God could do the impossible, and neither did she consider the consequences of her actions. The child of promise, Isaac, was the child God promised to Sara and Abram, and he was born on God's time.

One of my earlier experiences was with some of the older Christian women. They were stressing to the younger sisters that our obligation was to *fix ourselves* while in all circumstances, implying that would resolve a marriage gone wrong. If the husband is verbally, mentally, and physically abusive, whatever is ailing him, their advice was, "You just keep fixing yourself, tough it out; it'll get better." Unknowingly, they were advocating acceptance of abuse. Not knowing any better, neither questioning nor searching the truth for yourself, it's easy to fall for this type of misinterpreted teaching. God speaks to us in every circumstance. Search for yourself.

To the contrary, it could easily be a control issue, pride, or mental impairment when a man thinks provocative language and physical aggression is a means of self-expression. Slander, demeaning, and assaulting to the point of debilitating a woman in order to validate herself is always inexcusable. This stands for women who beat up on their men as well. There are so many cases in the judicial system where mental instability is used as a reason to allow a man who has slaughtered his wife to death to go free. Mental illness is not an exception to being abusive. Women should decline to foster self-blame for another person's misbehaviors. People have to want to be fixed.

I married two men with similarities, and both were Christians. One husband was already double-minded, and the second became double-minded. Each spouse loved the idea of being connected to a spiritual woman, a woman of values different from their past relationships. In my case, as both husband's relationship with God changed and their hearts no longer aligned with His principles, so did their thought pattern and behavior change. Inevitably our natures collided, and the marriage relationships took a turn for the negative. In both relationships, I began to be penalized for my persona, and for the woman they already knew I was, a woman of God. The woman they admired enough to marry then became threatening to their manhood. My credentials that they once applauded were under the scrutiny of their judge and jury attitudes, and they were always looking for a fault or a wrong for which to condemn me.

In both situations, I was blessed to have the influence of God's unconditional love and the satisfaction in knowing He foresees and does what is best in spite of the direction I was going. He wouldn't allow strongholds to conquer me and sustained me through my mistakes. There is one thing I can say for certain, and that is when God teaches you a lesson, it is hard to forget. After that, I have been adamant about listening and knowing when God is speaking to me. In fact, if there is such a thing, sometimes I think I am overly conscious. *"Be still and know that I am God." Psalms 46:10 (KJV)*

Chapter 9

They Rose Above the Shadow of Their Father

Often times, children are the ones who are most affected by an unhealthy relationship. Consequently, it isn't easy to be transparent about my children, but it is necessary, and it's the foundation for the existence of *Walking in the Shadow of a Schizophrenic/Power of Forgiveness.* My children's fortitude, character, and faith in an undesirable burden is exemplified. It is here that I share how relationships are contingent on the ability and heart to forgive, forgiveness of their stepdad.

Separately, I ask my three children their concerns for my writing this book. Each one had an interesting approach and response to the question. Knijel said, "Momma, I don't care if you write the book as long as it makes some money, but if it doesn't..." and we laughed. Tameka didn't have much to say, but I knew she was proud of me and okay with it. Aaron questioned, "Momma, are you not worried anymore about how Tameka and Knijel feel?" My response was, "If it's God's purpose and will, He will fix the hearts of everyone involved." Over time and with surmountable prayers, I was inspired to uncover our story. I promised God whatever happened in my life, good or bad, I would use it as a testimony to help others and to glorify Him.

Before I continue, however, I was led by the Spirit to be informative about the power of sex and how it needs careful consideration because it's a byproduct of how we bring children into this world. My discussion of it here lays a foundation for the transparencies of sexuality in our family that I'm sharing about later in the chapter. Sex is a unique, purposeful, and powerful design of God.

1). Sex is a unique fulfillment design by the Creator, God. 2). Sex was designed for marriage pleasure and is one of the most enjoyable and intimate physical needs of a man and woman in the realm of marriage. 3). Sex is powerful because it is designed not only to feel good, but it is the phenomenal physiology of procreation of children. Carefully read the following paragraph, for my intentions about this subject aren't judgmental.

To All Single Women and Men

The society we live in is full of deception, and people looking for something or someone to validate who they are. These people are looking for someone to bring fulfillment to their lives that only they can find, and God can give. To all single people, be careful who you allow to lie down beside you and to whom you pledge your life. That man or woman will either bring joy and peace into you and your children's life or pure hell.

My children are the most important thing in this world and were a joy for me to raise. My desire and goals were always to give them a better home life than I was accustomed to. I wanted the foundation for our stability to be Christianity, family-oriented, and experience of social fun and fulfillment as we worshipped together. Most parents don't deliberately and intentionally set out to hurt their children. I couldn't fathom me, a mother, an educator, supporter, and protector of little people could ever bring any harm to my children. So, you think. However, it happens. As I mentioned earlier, I made my first mistake at age sixteen, when I lived with the father of my two daughters. Brutally, I learned the hard way that having a child by a man doesn't mean he would make a good husband or father. Although Edward was baptized wouldn't mean a definite change inwardly. He was hot-tempered, controlling, a potty mouth, physical abuser, a man needy for a woman, and one who never learned how to appreciate and treat a woman. You see, I was blinded to those facts in our relationship prior to marrying him and didn't realize it was already toxic. I was young and unmindful of *"two wrongs don't make a right.* No matter how much shielding we do to protect our children in chaotic surroundings, they are touched and affected. This is a problem too often forgotten by single parents. Hurtful as it was, life goes on. I embraced oneness, single parenting, and proceeded to plan our future.

After eight years of divorce, I met a gentleman who I perceived was my *soul mate* and a wonderful stepfather to my daughters.

This brings me to divulging part of my life that is analogous to a soap opera. The difference is the characters aren't celebrities and the storylines aren't fictional. It is the hard-core truth about inappropriate sexual behavior. Such occurrences are constantly broadcasted over social media and happening at places and with people whom you least expected. It could be neighbors, schools, childcare centers, churches, parents, relatives, friends, caretakers, religious people, and leaders alike. When Satan can't deter you from your spiritual journey, viciously, he attacks the most *precious* thing to you, and for me, it was my children.

A couple of months after relocating to Danville, IL, I received a phone call from the school counselor at Danville Elementary School.   In my wildest dream, I wasn't expecting to hear such distressing news. The move to Danville was to distance me from a bitter situation. Instead, it was like having an old wound, thinking it has healed only to find out later, you've had a flare-up from infection. The counselor reported my younger daughter, Knijel, said she had been touched by her stepdad more than once, and Child Protective Services had been contacted. My heart began to beat fast, and my chest felt heavy; the feeling in my stomach was an indescribable churning partnered with lightheadedness. Besides the grief for Tameka and Knijel, I was engulfed with disappointment at myself. My girls hadn't made it home from school and so I had much time to self-reflect. This was another disaster due to the decisions I made, and the shadow came to Danville to inhabit my home. The man I loved and deeply believed was safe for my daughters to be around had betrayed me by doing the worse imaginable, besides physically killing them.

After the girls came home from school, I had gained some composure. I had to know. I pulled my oldest daughter, Tameka, near my side and asked, "Has your daddy been touching you?" She replied, "Yes." I held both my babies tight while assuring them everything was going to be alright. Realistically, I knew all was not going to be well. Would we survive this? Yes, I was confident.

Rose Kennedy wrote, *"Time heals all wounds."* I am not sure exactly what Mrs. Kennedy had in mind when she made this statement, but I didn't quite agree. My pain was like a keloid above the skin, visible at all times. Time may merely lessen the pain, but that dreadful day my heart told me this was nothing that was going away, and neither did I know what lied ahead for the girls. I had been in the business of teaching too long and had observed and experienced this trauma in other children. Children who are sexually invaded and exploited in any manner are left with some type of scars. Never did I entertain the thought of it happening to my babies. Even writing this chapter caused me to go through some withdrawals because recalling the pain I caused my children was colossal. Each time I set at the computer, I relived that day over and over. It was painful rehashing the counselor's voice, not to the full extent of what my body went through, such as the brokenness and the emotional suffering of my girls. However, it was still enough to shut me down with moments of sighs, tears, and groaning disappointment with myself. I was led to pray, "Lord, please help me get through this chapter."

Not for a moment, knowingly nor intentionally, would I allow any man to hurt my children, and yet it was a reality. I couldn't erase the anguish from their lives. God knows I learned later on what _forgiveness_ is not. I was glad to be in Danville when I found out they had been molested; at the time, the fewer people who knew was a positive for working toward healing. My daughters and I went through professional counseling, and the Pastor and the members of Collett Street Church were a great support system.

Amazingly, my children have the same personalities in adulthood as they did as children. Tameka is "Strength under Control," Knijel is the "Feisty Withstander," and Aaron is an "Adventurous Daredevil." This is what I saw in the three of them when they were young, and to this day, these traits still exist.

My Daughter, Tameka

Tameka majored in criminal justice. She works as a Circuit Court Deputy in the Domestic Violence/Family Court at the Hall of Justice in Louisville, Kentucky. She is a mother of two children, Kaelin and Justin, and has two grandchildren, Justin Jr., and Justice. Tameka is beautiful inside and out. She is independent and a hard worker. Her countenance depicts the type of heart she possesses. She is sacrificial, multi-talented, creative, has great teaching abilities, sings like a mockingbird, and has attributes of joy, compassion, and gratitude. She is playful and full of hilarious comments and jokes. With all of the wonderful qualities, there is another side of Tameka. When crossed, her anger can be just as strong as the beauty within. Tameka is a deeply caring and protective young woman, a little bit of a perfectionist, with mother wit, she meets no strangers and overly lavishes people with love.

One Christmas Day, Tameka set a box in my lap. Excitedly, I opened the plain white box and took out a beautiful peach hooded jacket. I wasn't a fan of jogging suits, and so at first glance, I was semi-happy, thinking it was an ordinary peach jacket. I responded with expressions of gratitude, "Awe...thank you, Tameka." However, it wasn't until I turned the jacket to the back that I lost it. On the back of the jacket was a picture of my three grandchildren who I was forced to hand over to Child Protective Services. Whenever Tameka does something for anyone, she's already considered their personality, what's taking place with them at the moment, then she goes out of her way to do the unexpected to make them happy. That's who she is.

The Voice of Tameka

"I can't remember how I felt as a child. I just know at night after church when we went home, I thought—who was going to protect us? I didn't understand why we went back. I don't know why I didn't tell someone about the abuse when it happened. *(Tameka alluded to me being a hard sleeper.)* It didn't happen right away, but negative behaviors surfaced. Feelings came out when I became an adult, and I began to hallucinate and have flashbacks of Daddy coming into the room. I stayed back in my bedroom, isolating myself from Derrick, (husband), and the boys. I was introverted and allowed people to mistreat me. I observed myself self-destruct in ways I allowed myself to be treated by others. I allowed others to impose on me, and I did not use my voice to fight back. Because I didn't tell anyone about the molestation when it happened, it's possibly why I didn't speak up or correct people immediately when they wronged me. I waited until later, and then I exploded. I overly lavished people with gifts and my love when they were neither deserving nor returned the love and favors. God helped me to work through all my issues, to love me, to <u>speak</u> for me, to care for me, and to put me first. My therapist and others, of whom I shared my situation, couldn't understand why I did not blame you, Momma. In fact, my therapist said I would in time. I chose not to blame. The only thing I know is God kept me from being the opposite of what I could have been."

I witnessed her forgiving spirit, another example of Tameka. On her wedding day, she chose Dallas over her biological father to walk her down the aisle. It was an act of grace and mercy that only God can place in the heart. Tameka loves Dallas and still addresses him as Daddy. She knows despite his <u>heinous</u> sin against her, Dallas loves her. I recall her commenting, *"The way that Daddy loves us..."* My *heart leaped* when I heard these spoken words from her mouth. I knew she meant a *"healthy love."*

In 2016, near the Fourth of July, Tameka took her sons, Kaelin, Justin, and her grandson, Justin Jr. to Oxmoor Lodge to visit with her daddy. She took pictures of him and the boys and placed them on her Facebook page. Tameka said to me, "I am not ashamed of Daddy. I put him on Facebook, and everyone who knew him and hadn't seen him in a long time liked the picture and said they were glad to know that Brother Dallas was doing fine."

Although Tameka so gracefully said to me, "I chose not to blame." I absolutely am the blame. In her sudden absence, there were spurts of hurt. Times she was distant, and I felt I was being punished. If so, I had no right to speculate, place pressure upon her, or have a pity party. I accepted it. I took responsibility for being a party to her pain. I saw behaviors I knew were out of Tameka's character. As much as I desired to, I couldn't be that mother hen to pull her under my wing. She was no longer my first adorable baby who merely had a bruise in which I could wash and apply a band-aid to make it better.

Tameka's relationship and faith in God worked in her to extend love, which is also a specialty of her personhood. She grew into a strong and resilient young woman.

My Daughter, Knijel

Knijel majored in the medical field and obtained an Associate Degree in Medical Assistance, PCA. She is a patient care associate at Norton Suburban Hospital in Louisville, Kentucky. Knijel is the mother of three children who are Braxton (deceased), Damond Jr., and Diamond. She is more of a fashionista with a passion for shoes and purses. She is my beautiful chocolate girl who is feisty, mouthy, candid, out-spoken, ill-tempered, and emotional to the point that she gets roused over problems that don't involve her and, in an instant, can go from 0-10. She is tenacious, independent, works hard, is self-willed, and persistent toward anything she sets her mind to do. Knijel is independent, a go-getter, and knows how to handle her business. She has multiple talents and potential, which she tends to withhold. She is adventurous and likes traveling and having a good time. Knijel wears and talks a tough exterior, but inwardly has a big heart. She is one of my children who, every now and then, blew my mind with the wisdom that flowed from her mouth.

The Voice of Knijel

"I don't remember a whole lot when I was little. I remember when Daddy sat me on his lap. I remember inappropriate things he would say to me over the phone, even as I grew older. I recall times he exposed himself to me, which he did when you were gone."

When Dallas and I were separated, Knijel wrote a letter that was very explicit regarding her feelings about him and his approach to her. She brought it to me. I believe some of her trust issues and relationships are repercussions from the molestation. Over the years, she retreated from Dallas and me. She has displayed anger, rebellion, and hatred in many ways.

Although she has uttered some pretty hurtful and sharp words, there hasn't been one time in our conversations or disagreements that I have ever once speculated nor doubted her love for me. I soon got over the hurt because I am the blame. I dealt with it by deciphering what I was not going to take and internalizing it with what was truth and what I deserved. She had a right to vent, and I needed to listen if that meant I had to be the one taking the darts. I stayed focused on what I knew to be a fact. My daughter trusted me and knew that I have been there and always will be. Unpleasant as may be, we can talk honestly and openly about the past.

It has been interesting over the years to observe how strongly she feels whenever she speaks the word, Daddy. She is referring to Dallas and not her biological father. She knows she can depend on him, and most imperative, behind that distorted mindset, he loves her in a *"healthy way"* the way a father should. She didn't go into detail but voiced to me that after many years in 2014, Dallas apologized to her, despite what she still thinks about him and the anger flares.

Dallas and schizophrenia live in the same house as Knijel, and she is his caregiver. Past experience has taught her how to live with her father's illness and its triggers. When he pushes her last nerve, Knijel's temperament arises, and she goes off on him, but she will not allow anyone else that prerogative. She doesn't approve of his hygiene, is most tolerable, and she's not ashamed to take him in public. She laughs at him in a loving way by embracing some things he enjoys, such as knowing what music he likes. Periodically and especially on one particular Father's Day, Knijel played his favorite Michael Jackson CD, titled, "Billie Jean," just to watch him dance. I am proud of Knijel and grateful that the barriers that were between all of us are no longer there. We worked through them.

My Son, Aaron

Dallas made this remark about our son's character, "Aaron has some of you and me in him, and that's a hell of a combination. Like both of us, when he believes in something, he doesn't change unless it is shown to him."

The name Aaron was a perfect fit for him, meaning *"mountain,"* which correlated with his life's journey.

Aaron is short in stature, handsome, smart, and has a calm nature. He is the father of four, Da'Janae, Amuri, Nathaniel, and MaKaury. My pregnancy with Aaron was entertaining. It was like packing around a boxing champion. My dress or shirt bounced up and down from the constant hard kicks. It was a signal to me that he was going to be rambunctious. One day when Aaron was eleven months old, I was sitting on the couch heavily into some reading, and I momentarily looked up to check on him. Aaron was dangling on the outside edge of the stair rail on the second floor. His little hands were gripping tightly to the ledge, and his chubby little body was twisting as his tiny feet swayed from beneath his gown. Grasping tightly to the rails, never once did he whimper, indicate fear, nor expressed a need to be rescued. Quickly and gently, I placed my hands around his waist, lowered him down and gave him hugs and kisses. Tickled, I asked, "How did you get on the other side of this rail?"

Between the ages of three and four, Aaron was still engaging in parallel and solitary play. When his playmates surrounded him, Aaron had his own interest, creative play, and was content playing alone. It wasn't until he would soon turn six that he blossomed into an adventurous and exploratory little person. If I could give a visual description of Aaron in words, it would be taken from the television show, *To Tell the Truth*. He displayed a passive spirit, not always because he wanted to do so. Interestingly, Aaron and his sister Tameka were similar in that aspect, of which they both had to grow out of their passive spirits, unlike Knijel, who is totally the opposite and will hardly let anything slip by her. On the other hand, like Tameka, Aaron can be just as tough as he is passionate when pushed to a level.

He enjoyed writing at an early age and was very good at it. In elementary school, Aaron won a number of medals and Author Award Certificates, two books of which I remember were titled, *The Tiger who Lost Its Stripes* and *The Magic Dishes*. Dallas and I were in awe at when Walt Disney's *Beauty and the Beast* came to the theatres. The dishes in the movie were similar to the magic dishes Aaron wrote about in his book. As Aaron grew older, he developed a phobia for speaking in front of people. Consequently, any other extracurricular program he took part in became a threat if he had to stand before the class or perform. For instance, he enjoyed the youth Black Achievers Program until he was asked to do a presentation. After that request, he lost interest in the program.

Aaron received his high school diploma while incarcerated. Through Blue Grass Academy, he learned several trades such as carpentry, electrician, welding, lawn service,

HVAC, among other trade skills. His aspiration has always been to become a barber and to open his own business. Whenever he was incarcerated, he used his barber skills. The irony is my curiosity to know how much he was making to cut hair for inmates. When I asked, his response was absolutely amusing. He said, one to two dollars or a honey bun. I couldn't contain my laughter at the thought of him working for that little amount in jail but had a tough time with small paying jobs on the outside. Aaron lacked the motivation for holding down a regular job due to straying from home at age fourteen and being involved in a promiscuous environment. He spiraled down a wayward path, which led to indulging in drug dealing and fast money, not realizing *easy money* comes with a set of problems and definitely not without a price.

Yes, it was hard to admit he was such a troubled child. A mental health doctor informed me that the second or third child most likely could be affected by schizophrenia, and signs of the illness are normally exhibited between the ages of 19-22 years old. Of course, it concerned me since Aaron was Dallas's second child. A consolation was that I knew Aaron inherited some of my genes. Aaron surpassed the age variable for any symptoms, and I was grateful schizophrenia wasn't a part of his life. Even though Aaron was not stricken physically by schizophrenia, however, the illness was a major part of his upbringing.

It wasn't until his late twenties he revealed to me the effects of our family problems. He said, "When you and daddy would argue, I didn't know who to believe. It just toughened me. I always felt alone."

During a short altercation with his dad, Aaron sternly affirmed, "When you left, where was I to go? Who was going to teach me how to be a man?" He endured and dealt with incomprehensible behaviors of his dad's mental state. Ambitious, adaptive, refined, nonconformist, and nobility are descriptions of our son's journey.

In the face of bullying, Aaron managed to adapt/survive the mockery, laughter, and cruel names toward his dad by peers. At home, he experienced a revolving door dad and an absentee dad at school. A once committed church dad became indifferent. When his dad was present, Aaron tolerated loud outbursts, distorted language, weird looks, and witnessed a parent so different from other dads.   Clueless to the directionality of manhood, Aaron was *ambitious* and determined to explore the world and all its treasures. And in doing so, he became fearless.

Over the years, while life took its toll, beat him up, and at the same time *refined* him, early Biblical teaching kept him intact. I received various letters from him while he was in prison regarding his spiritual feeling. One specifically read, "Momma, I am thankful you taught me about God, or I probably would have been crazy.

Aaron once shared with me one day the realization he wasn't the only one with a dysfunctional family and that his peers had problems and issues going on too. Aaron savored good memories as well. He had recollections of time spent with his dad and how he supported, provided for him, and effortlessly tried to intercept him from troubled situations, regardless, of what he needed most, male guidance, and companionship were lacking. I endeavored to partner Aaron with male mentors like "Big Brothers" and "Sons of Israel." These programs were efficient and impactful, but for every male child filling the dad role is not easy, and neither is it successful. Biological dads are hard to replace.

The Voice of Aaron

Perhaps unified hearts prevented the rush to reveal the girl's molestation to Aaron. Also, neither was I ever pressed by my daughters to tell Aaron about the perverseness of his dad. I shuddered at the fact it would be devastating for him to face his sisters. After all, this was his biological father. Just the same, he needed to know, and I told him. The silence was broken with Aaron asking, "Momma, how did you come to accept it? I just had a penknife stuck into my heart." He had every right to ask anything of me, and in response, I explained, "Aaron, I didn't know. I would never knowingly allow anyone to hurt Tameka and Knijel. As for going back and living in the same house with your dad, all I can say is that over time it left my mind." Instinctively, I knew Aaron would suffer in silence.

There is no doubt there was disappointment in his dad, yet he showed no signs of hatred or ill-feelings toward him. If he did, I never witnessed it. He was more concerned about his dad's welfare. "Momma, tell Pop, hi. Tell Daddy, I love him. Momma, is Daddy sick? Does

Daddy need to go to the hospital?" He volunteered to become a part of caretaking for his dad under state guardianship.

I knew Aaron was adventuresome and dauntless. I just didn't know how much until he became the *Prodigal Son.* He hadn't quite reached the spiritual peak of maturity, for he continued to wrestle with avoiding the street life or to allow God's way to become his. On many occasions, I listened through his tears of grief because he felt trapped, "It's hard, Momma." I encourage every parent not to give up, and when you talk to God about your child, pray with expectancy, know that no matter how long it takes, a change will come.

One Last Time

In October 2019, Aaron was paroled with nine months left on the shelf. Unlike most times in the past, when he was paroled or released from jail within less than two months, he was back on familiar territory, behind bars.

Glory to God, Aaron maintained contact with his Parole Officer and made it through the nine months. He was a free man. With his slick as grease moves, he didn't fool me. He still dibbled and dabbled here and there with pushing drugs and mingling with the same people who dealt him a bad hand. It didn't stop me. I don't know if I could have called on God any more than I did over the years. I never ceased my prayers and supplication for him.

"God, keep him. Father, break him. Let Your will become his. Lord, let him have a personal experience as Jacob in the Bible who wrestled with an angel. Let Aaron wrestle with an angel until he is submissive."

After twenty-two years of praying God's protection, grace, and mercy over my son, I began to see small changes. As a Christian woman in this spiritual race, I knew change doesn't come easy, and neither does it come overnight. Genuine change takes time. I could not let up from praying for him for I knew Satan would work harder to grab hold to him. Late one night, Aaron came to my apartment. As he stood in the hallway, I observed the grayish tone of his skin, sagging puppy dog eyes, and he seemingly dropped weight in a week. My son looked worn, tired, and lifeless. As he leaned against the wall, he began to rub the top of his head in a circular motion then he said, "I'm dying momma. It hurts to change. Do you think I need something spiritual? Momma, I'm done with the streets; I'm not going back out there." He broke into tears. My heart bled.

It was November 17, and shortly after Aaron's visit that I was awakened by a song on my ringtone. Gazing at the phone, I noticed it was three o'clock in the morning and wondered who could be calling? Still half asleep, I was able to focus my eyes on a 585 number, which was all too familiar. I went into a deep sigh as I listened to Aaron speak in a descending tenor. Frustrated, I asked, "Are you in jail." He filled my head with an explanation while reassuring me he was locked up over a traffic violation. Jail was jail and one more time was still too much. During his twenty-day stay in Shelby County Detention Center, I received many calls from Aaron acknowledging God and sharing dreams he'd encountered while in his cell. He would often ask me what they meant and explained to me what he felt God was doing with his spirit.

As frustrated as I was with him, it took one last time for the Lord to bound Aaron with spiritual shackles to bring him to the point of listening and being receptive to His Spirit. Aaron experienced multiple visions to bring unrest to his hardheaded spirit prompting him to seek answers the street couldn't deliver. In the meantime, Satan was declaring war on my son's thought process by tempting him to believe things were happening when they really weren't. Aggravated about his cronies and circumstances for which he had no control, he was on the verge of having a meltdown. A cellmate calmed him by warning him that he was going to drive himself crazy. God has prison angels, too, who helped free Aaron of the strongholds. Don't allow Satan's blows to take you out.

December of 2019 will forever be a memorial, it's the month and the year my son died.   Early in the morning, I received a call from the Shelby County Detention Center, which left me rejoicing. Aaron was in confession mode. He began telling me of more dreams and visions. He saw through spiritual eyes. After we hung up, I moved to the living room, which was a serene atmosphere where the Christmas lights surrounded the wise men statues, and there I shouted, "Thank you, Jesus." over and over.

One last time Aaron locked away with himself to face who he really was in comparison to the person he had portrayed for so long. One last time brought focus and clarity, which prompted him to call me at 3:58 am excited to tell me what God revealed to him in the dreams. "Momma, I'm writing a book about my life." He read two chapters of what he wrote, and it was evident he had writing skills. Following reading the chapters, he asked a question that absolutely blew me away, "Momma, are you going to pray with me? My son just asked me to pray with him and for me to give him scriptures to save on his iPhone.

Aaron was released from the detention center and came directly to my apartment. Since I wasn't at home, he left a letter on my nightstand that had an illustration of a heart with a cross in the middle. It read,

"I love you, my Lady. There are never enough words or expressions to share with someone who is as GRAND a Queen of God's compassion and vision. We're winning Momma, my conflictions refined."

The letter ended with a drawing of an eye with a teardrop flowing from the corner. Praise God for one last time. The Prodigal Son came home.

Memories of Self Expressions

Words cannot express the respect and love I have for my children, and all they have gone through due to a decision I made. Far-reaching is their love, and they have expressed it in words.

"Momma, for all that you've been through, seen, experienced, figured out, have done, taught, <u>slept</u> through (Lol), you always seemed to be able to strive, succeed, fall and get back up, motivate, and persevere. As your daughter, I've watched, listened, and a lot of times rebelled against you. No matter what, you never give up. You truly are a blessing and more. I don't know if I'll ever be able to fill your shoes. I am sincerely grateful to have you as my mother. Love Always, Knijel"

I replied, "God has a pair of shoes for you; all you have to do is wear them."

"Everything I need to know about real generosity of spirit, I learned from you, Mom. You know it's true, there's lots of favor still on your life." Thank you,

Momma, for teaching me about God. Love you, Tameka."

Excerpts from Aaron's letters and emails from prison:

"I'm thinking about going all out and being the son

u raised me to be…Thank you for always believing in me

and never giving up, plus being firm. I need you always,

even in my darkness. To this present moment, I reminisce

about my childhood memories, wanting you to know I

cherish you to the fullest. Without you, I would be a very

troubled man. You passed the God in you to me and our

family, which keeps me grounded, hindering that part of me

that hasn't been destructive. You are great. I love you,

Momma 4 EVA. I appreciate your impeccable strength.

There is never a time I've witnessed you give up or let go,

especially on God. Things I heard you speak and seen

reminds me of the story of Job. I trust and believe at the

end of this unfortunate journey (in the now), God has

something beautiful, fulfilling, and joyous in store that

makes your struggle so worth it. He recognizes your faith and willingness to wait upon Him (Honor). You are such a blessing. Honestly, Momma, I long to have that side of you. Thank you, Aaron."

On my worst days, my children made me feel like the woman Lemuel's mother described in the book of Proverbs 31, "Her children rise up and call her blessed." There are days when I am plagued, from time to time, with constant reminders by a spiritual message, books, conversations, movies, etc. For Dallas, speaking on the molestation was difficult to draw from that "deep well," and typically, he shut down. Once, he did manage to say, "I am glad nothing more happened." Hopefully, he wasn't minimizing touching.

In 2014 during a conversation, I was so thankful to hear Knijel's voice. "Daddy and I had a talk, and after all these years, he had never said he was sorry. He apologized." Enabling me to publicly tell our story says much for my children's resilience and their character. Descriptive of my family, is the Bible scripture, "*iron sharpens iron.*" When you rub together two iron blades, both blades are sharpened. Together we strengthened one another. Have my children ever thrown me under a bus? Uh, yeah. Just keeping it real.

Kudos to my grandchildren, nieces, and nephews who gracefully put up with Dallas's moods and long lectures, although they knew he stood guilty of his very words. Blank expressions on their faces were an indication they were getting annoyed, yet they remained respectful and listened and never made fun of him. In fact, they laughed with him. Without totally understanding their granddaddy, they understood he had a serious sickness and equipping them with knowledge of the illness, they were aware Satan and schizophrenia were working together and were the culprits.

Chapter 10

Grace and Mercy Saved Me from Me

Maintaining Christian composure when it comes to safeguarding our children is easier said than done. Natural reflexes are derived from an inherent nature to protect our children. In a matter of seconds, fears and impulses can turn into an emotional upheaval and temperament, driving a sane person to insanity and to inflict pain on another.

I laid in the recliner, watching Dallas lying in bed, slumbered in a deep sleep. My state of mind had no place for empathy of his illness, gnashing of the teeth, and periodic rage overshadowed me. I felt only shame, detest, and kindled anger for what he had done to my daughters. The rage inside sufficed me taking a semi-automatic firearm and shooting as many rounds it took to satisfy my displeasure and hostility. Frankly, I don't know if I had enough nerve to fire a weapon; nonetheless, I pictured myself going through the motion. It took a length of time to rid my mind of the thoughts of blowing him away.

I didn't have the capabilities to do it alone; only God can eradicate thoughts of this magnitude. I am thankful for an Omnipresent God when evil succumbs to our thoughts. *"Do you not know? Have you not heard? The Lord is the everlasting God, the Creator of the ends of the earth. He will not grow tired or weary, and his understanding no one can fathom. He gives strength to the weary and increases the power of the weak."*

"Even youths grow tired and weary, and young men stumble and fall, but those who hope in the Lord will renew their strength. They will soar on wings like eagles; they will run and not grow weary they will walk and not be faint." Isaiah 40:28-31 (NIV).

Staring at the eagle pictures and figurines on the glass shelves, I gained endurance during those trying times. I stood in awe of that magnificent bird's wing capacity to fly above the storms for safety, and their ability to see danger more clearly than any other winged creature. Eagles are a pillar of strength and a reminder that God empowers us to succeed above any storms in our lives. I refused to allow predators of pain, anger, revenge, and an unforgiving spirit to overtake me, which could have precipitated murder. I couldn't allow anger to lead to regret; no person or situation was worth that price. My feet didn't tread where I could have gotten access to a weapon. My unwholesome thoughts and strongholds took refuge in reading the Bible, prayer, meditation, and worship was a remote place. It was my inner sanctuary, a place where I not only found peace, but my convictions were ever before me.

There were too many times to count that my mind wandered over the scripture verse, *"Be ye angry, and sin not: let not the sun go down upon your wrath: " Ephesians 4:26 (KJV)*. What was more disturbing, Dallas couldn't come to terms with the contempt I had, and his unwillingness to connect with mine and our children's pain was a sure indication of internal shadows. The word of God kept rage under control. The destructive seed that provoked my mind to place me in harm's way or cause reckless behavior in the life of another was removed. *"That ye might walk worthy of the Lord unto all pleasing, being fruitful in every good work, and increasing in the knowledge of God. Strengthened with all might, according to his glorious power, unto all patience and longsuffering with joyfulness..." Colossians 1:10-11 (KJV).*

"You"

My life was NOTHING

You brought JOY into my spirit

You gave PEACE as I faced my darkest fears

You gave back to me LAUGHTER in the midst of my failures

You breathe WISDOM in times of uncertainties

You provided FRIENDSHIP in the nick of time.

You held up my HEAD

You EMBRACED and KEPT me wrapped in truth

You Lord, I yearn to spend eternity

Foreknowledge and Providence of God

"Before I formed thee in the belly, I knew thee…" *Jeremiah 1:5 (KJV).* He predestinated us before the foundation of the world. *Romans 8:29-30 (NLT) "I know the plans I have for you, declares the Lord, plans to prosper you and not to harm you, plans to give you a hope and a future." Jeremiah 29:11 (NIV) "…it judges the thoughts and attitudes of the heart." Hebrew 4:12 NIV)*

He is the Creator and Ruler of the Universe, and in all things, He has a hand in both good and the bad. God knows the intent of the heart and every motive behind human actions. Therefore, He desires faith. The Bible states, *"…If you have faith as small as a mustard seed…" Matthew 17:20 (NASB)* The Holy Spirit works with whatever amount of faith one owns. Should our faith level continue to be small or remain the same? I think not. Eventually, our faith should grow and develop through trials, and the trials ought to invigorate our faith and elevate our trust in a faithful God. It is then that life's impossibilities become possible.

Personal Calling

No matter how hard I tried to distance myself or the length of time apart, I could not get beyond Dallas's shadow. Whenever my husband was around folks, college campus, store, walking the streets, etc., I was guaranteed to receive a call from someone, or law enforcement, regarding him being a menace. While living in Danville, I remained in touch with family and friends by occasionally traveling to Louisville to attend functions at the College of the Scriptures and the Annual Christian Women's Retreat. During my travels back to Louisville, I didn't anticipate rearranging or shifting plans. However, once there, I found myself walking in my husband's shadows again. No sooner than I stepped foot in the city, I would get a call from someone inquiring about Dallas's whereabouts. He often disappeared. One thing for sure, many concerned people loved him and usually let me know when he was in trouble. Knowing him, people who knew Dallas consciously felt some kind of way when he was in a psychotic state. I later learned that Dallas was off medication and mysteriously disappeared and hadn't been seen over four months. I contacted his immediate family, church family, shelters, county jail, and visited his apartment before finding out he had been admitted to the VA Hospital. Upon returning home from Louisville, I made sure his rent was paid up so he would have a place to live after being discharged from the hospital.

A few months after one of my visits, I planned to travel to Atlanta for the women's retreat with a stopover at the College of the Scriptures in Louisville to pick up a group of ladies. Upon my arrival, rumors that Dallas had been missing were shot at me like an archer shooting a quiver of arrows. The bus arrived at the college late at night, and the only means of communication was a payphone outside the men's dorm. After settling in, I gathered a few dimes to make some calls to familiar places I knew Dallas might have gone, and the last resort was the city jail. Before leaving Louisville, I was relieved to know that Dallas had been incarcerated for 14 days. Considering his state of mind, the jail was safer than drifting in the streets.

Fortunately, I was able to speak with a compassionate jail clerk who informed me of Dallas's mental state. So that his awkwardness wouldn't be taken as intentional behavior, I explained that I would return to Louisville and take care of the arrangements for him to be released. Following my trip, I remained in Louisville to start what I knew to be a lengthy process of hiring an attorney to get temporary Power of Attorney and to hire a criminal lawyer. In a week, Dallas was released from jail and placed in his home away from home care at the VA Hospital. I always knew to check on the status of his rent situation, which was a major issue when he was off his medication. He had no consciousness of bills. His bills were paid, and I returned home to Illinois as planned. Repetitive and time-consuming as it was, I felt compelled to do the right thing by him.

Chapter 11

Marriage Metamorphosis

My marriage changed more times than I care to remember. Unlike the caterpillar that wraps itself into a cocoon and eventually comes out a beautiful butterfly, our marriage never seemed to reach that stage. When Dallas was off his medicine, he had monopolizing personalities each of which he selfishly demanded my time, attention, and affection. He was intimidating and persistent on having his way and acted as a law unto himself. He set standards for himself and for the world. No doubt, the rules for himself were lenient and critical with no leniency for the rest of us. Spiritual principles only applied to him when they fit his purpose, but he governed the entire world by them.

During my entire time away from Dallas, I could sense the energy of him pestering and demanding family, friends, and church family to reveal where we relocated. It was a matter of time until he would map his way to the city. His trips became frequent, and he would visit Collett Street Church on Sunday knowing the children and were sure to be there. The more he visited, the more at eased I became and felt comfortable enough to allow my Dallas to take our son, Aaron, to Louisville for a week.

One Sunday morning, Dallas unexpectedly showed up to worship. He apologetically came before the church and with, supposedly, a repented spirit. Neither his confession nor the apology struck me as being genuine, for I had been free of him for some time now and I wasn't in the mood to deal with him or our relationship. The facial expressions can speak volumes, and apparently mine exhibited what I was feeling on the inside, not knowing I was being read.

Following worship, my mentor, Sister Tillman, came for a visit, and she had a serious look. Her glasses would twitch on her nose when she wanted to tell me something of importance. Sister Tillman chattered on and on saying things like, *"Girl, I looked over at you, and I thought, what is wrong with her. This man is up there pouring his heart out…"* I had no answer other than I wasn't ready, nor was I certain I'd ever wanted to pursue a relationship with him again.

Soon I surrendered to his pleas for forgiveness and thought perhaps we could work on the relationship and marriage. After some time, I made the decision for us to return to Louisville as a couple. My children were ecstatic about going home to see familiar faces we abruptly left behind. Back in Louisville, we huddled in Dallas's two-bedroom apartment and resided there until we got a larger place. After two months, our new home had three bedrooms, two-baths, and a balcony at Bent Creek Apartments. Moving day was tiresome, and by nightfall our only concern was putting up the beds. Once the children were bedded down for the night, with the little ounce of strength Dallas and I had left, we managed to put up our bed.

Like most couples who had distanced themselves, we weren't too tired for intimacy. We made love and laid alongside each other with hands clasped, as tears streamed down my cheeks. Dallas gently kissed the tears from my face. Truly I was glad to be home. After a night of passion, my expectations the morning after were nothing short of happiness and moving forward. I opened my eyes to the brightness of daylight filtering through the open blinds. With my blue pastel sheet blocking my view, I pulled it from my face as I lifted my head from the pillow and witnessed a horrifying scene.

A look of familiarity and an estranged figure was standing on the side of the bed, looking directly at me. A look of trouble. A look of sickness. I was in a daze while an immediate rush of thoughts went through my head,

"Should I have come home? What did I come back to?" I rose to my elbows to get a closer view of Dallas standing there. He stood speechless with a cross between a crazed smile and an erratic look. The external shadow that came to Danville was not as it appeared to be. Again, I felt betrayed by a façade. The internal shadow still ruled and controlled him, and he wasn't truthful regarding his medications. My emotions were high, and at the same time, I was low-spirited, embarrassed, and despondent with myself because I had returned with my children to the turmoil we once escaped.

God blessed me with the sweetest babies ever. The whiny and tantrum-throwing wasn't part of my children's make-up. Knowing we had to leave our home again, it broke my heart to tell them. Three months back in Louisville, not even one day in our new home, and then like a vagabond, I was looking for new living quarters. It wasn't going to work. So why put us through the longevity of issues. As much as it hurt, I needed to get out then. The only place I knew to retreat was with my sister, who lived fairly close. I made contact and asked if I could stay with her until I got a place of my own. Independence being part of my nature and preferring my own space without infringing on others, I would most definitely make it happen sooner than later.

The second week with my sister, she walked into the bedroom and said, "Brenda, I need my space and my privacy." Shocked, but I held it together, I replied, "Ok, I understand." I was broken, yet I refused to let my little ones see the waterfall on my face—not today. I didn't want to prolong my stay another day, so I called a friend who was like a biological sister and asked if I could stay with her. She welcomed my children and me. I checked the public transportation and began packing our belongings while explaining to my babies that we had to leave their aunt's home. Like any typical child, they questioned me but never complained. That's why I took snacks, books, drinks, coloring books, and crayons in a bag wherever we went to ensure they were entertained, comfortable, and mostly because they deserved it.

We walked the dark streets of the Lincoln Park neighborhood to the bus stop and caught the 5:30 am Appliance Park Bus to the Village West Apartments. I glanced over at my children sitting quietly, kicking their feet, and staring out the window into the night. Where we were about to move wasn't the safest place. Periodically during the night, I lay on the couch watching through the sheer white curtains as drug dealers transacted their business. I searched and compiled a list of job opportunities. Each morning between the hours of 8 a.m. and late into the evening, I rode the public transportation to unfamiliar parts of town to look for employment.

A few months later, one Friday afternoon, I arrived home from my job search around 2:30 p.m. and at 3:50

p.m., I received a call from Saint Joseph's Orphanage & Residential Child Development Center. The Director requested an interview the following Monday, and I was hired as a teacher at $3.50 an hour. You would have thought the pay wage was $35.00 an hour. I sat down and began calculating how much I could afford for an apartment I had already chosen to live in before getting employed. Things were looking up for me. I had my own income, a place to reside, and I was embarking on my career goal as an educator.

Starting over was not easy. I recalled times in the past when I left Danville and returned to Louisville to make a fresh start with expectations that things would be better for myself and children only to discover my husband was still the same man. So, this time, I had heart to heart talks with myself to encourage myself. There was a *power* that stood with me in Louisville. That same *power* was with me in Danville and will always be my shield. *"But thanks be to*

God, which giveth us the victory through our Lord Jesus

Christ. Therefore, my beloved brethren, be ye steadfast,

unmovable, always abounding in the work of the Lord,

forasmuch as ye know that your labor is not in vain in the

Lord." I Corinthians 15:57-58 (KJV)

Still Spinning

The phone rang, and shockingly the call was from New York. The gentleman introduced himself as a physician and told me Dallas was in New York and had been walking the streets with no shoes. Someone recognized he wasn't a resident and took him to the VA hospital. I replied that Dallas was originally from New York and had a sister who lived there, but now he resided in Louisville, KY. I assured him I would contact his immediate family in Louisville. Dallas's family reached out to his sister and made sure he was safe and flown back to Louisville so he could be admitted to the VA Hospital. It was nothing for Dallas to leave town without notice. Once, he pocketed $3,000 cash in his wallet and drove our GMC Jimmy, supposedly going to Cincinnati, but went from state to state instead only to find himself at the Canadian border. When he recognized where he was, he turned around and headed home. What took place during that trip I have no idea, and I am positive neither did he. It was a miracle he made it safely back to Louisville. And wouldn't you know it as soon as he returned to Louisville, the motor locked up. Talking about *divine intervention.*

I accepted behaviors that were detrimental such as hallucinations, delusions, manic episodes, and so forth due to the illness because these were actions beyond his control. Consequently, there were times I pondered who or what was the culprit? I had to differentiate between my husband's character, weaknesses, and the disease. I refused to feed into the behaviors which were due to him feeling himself and fulfilling the pleasures of his flesh. Friends and church family voiced their opinions, "Oh Brenda, he is just sick." Tell me something I didn't know. Love and compassion do not mean you remain blind.

I recall one beautiful Mother's Day morning when the men of the church prepared to show appreciation for mothers in the congregation. The women were called to the front by age groups and were to remain standing until all names had been announced. The older were given a red carnation and a card. My husband got up, went down the line, and hugged each woman. Okay, I could live with that. Next, the younger women were called and given a yellow carnation and a card. I sat there thinking. Surely, he's not going to repeat the same behavior. He knows it looks inappropriate. When my husband was anxious while sitting, he had a habit of shifting his body up and down.

Gently I placed my hand on his leg and whispered quietly, "Dallas, don't do this." His response was crushing. "Leave me alone." He proceeded to give each sister a hug, came back to the pew, and sat down beside me as if he had done nothing wrong. It hadn't registered, nor was he observant of the fact that he was the only man in the church who responded in this manner. I soon learned if my husband was bent on doing something, come hell and high waters, he didn't give it much thought or no thought. He did whatever came to mind. When we arrived home, I spoke about the incident. We further discussed respect and appropriateness. Another day, another conversation when the well was just too deep. Schizophrenia may have aided a little, but this was an act of the flesh, self-will, and self-gratification. One of the older sisters of the church smiled at me and sweetly said, "Brenda doesn't care; she gets hers at home." She meant well and may have tried to console me. She was oh so wrong, I did care. What he once valued in our relationship was diminishing.

Dallas caroused clubs, and more on Friday and Saturday nights, came to worship on Sunday morning and set on the front row still clothed in narcissism. Every now and then, Pastor's message touched on fornication, lasciviousness, reveling, and making provisions to sin. Dallas's body began to rise off the bench piercing the acoustics with his repeated shouts of "amen." Normally it was hard to divert my attention from the message, but not this Sunday. I was distracted by his voice bouncing off the sanctuary walls and him agreeing with Biblical truth and living the opposite, and knowing the members were aware of his double standards didn't make it any easier. Judgmental thoughts raced through my head while anger pressed me to turn the bench over on him. Dallas felt all should be accepting of his attitude and behaviors, even God. My husband was living a double standard, desensitized to the pain of others, and especially to our children and me. He was a good man troubled by so-o-o-o many bad spirits, and Satan capitalized on them all. Most puzzling, Dallas failed to understand Satan at work in our marriage and was intent on another family to self-destruct.

Whenever there is a family breakdown, it affects the church, community, society, and the world. Undeserving as I felt my husband was, and in my endeavors to avoid helping him, *agape love* was stronger, and compassion was the driving force that kept me coming to his aide. Agape love reminded me if it weren't for God's grace, it could be me. How often do we place our feet in the shoes of others?

People who had never been married, those who didn't quite understand my situation, felt they had a right to speak to my issues. These people were quick to tell me what I shoulda, coulda done, and what they woulda done. I shut out the "noise" of opinionated folks so I could hear God clearly and do what was right. I concluded that I had to base my decisions and my stewardship on what I could spiritually live with. I came to the conclusion, the highest good is to help those who can't help themselves. *"We walk by faith; not by sight." 2 Corinthians 5:7 (KJV)*

The Parable of the Good Samaritan teaches us what is honorable and meaningful to God, for his people to take on a spirit of servanthood and to spread love abroad.

> - To value human life

> - Leave our comfort zone

> - Accountability

> - Hospitality

> - Our neighbor is anyone with a need

> - True support isn't just giving money and materialism, but to give of oneself

> - It is unconditional love without expectation

"For if ye love them which love you, what reward have ye?" Matthew 5:46 (KJV)

Chapter 12

Be Careful What You Ask of God

The Creator created us to be *liberal thinkers* to make our *own choices.* The problems arise when our decisions and will do not align with His, and our choices are based on human and selfish ambitions or situations not carefully thought out. God welcomes us to come before Him to ask anything our heart so desires. Do we listen for the right answer, or do we listen for what feels close to what we already have made up in our minds to do?

Have you ever prayed to God for something, and when it happened, you've forgotten what you asked until He reminds you? I prayed to God on two separate occasions for specific things, and He answered my prayer.

Prayer One

God had already remedied my marital situation. Now I asked, "Lord, please allow Dallas and me to come together once again so that we can share what it's really like to live as husband and wife." Yes. Those were my exact words. God rendered my request just the way I asked. When we pray, the Devil is listening too, and he wants nothing more than to deter us from God's way. He also tries to misconstrue God's plan and divert His answer for our daily walk and future. The Devil pries his way into an already bad or unwise prayer request and is ready to create havoc and cause failure in our lives.

Let me explain what is meant by a bad prayer. Was it wrong to want a good marriage relationship? Of course not, but if the handwriting on the wall has given you clarity or its obvious your marriage partner doesn't have the capacity to love self, has some serious baggage, nor at the time is void of understanding the long-term meaning of the wedding vows. The marriage is already doomed or headed for failure, and it will not work. God had already shown me.

My two nephews and I lived in a rental house that didn't meet my expectations as a place I wanted to spend my life. I asked God for a home I could call my own with an affordable mortgage. My aspiration was a three-bedroom, two full baths, with a decent size front and back yard for the boys and grandchildren to enjoy. I talked with God about the neighborhood in which I wanted to live. Dallas and I had been separated for a while, with no plans of reconciling. However, I contacted him and asked if he would use his VA Government Loan assistance to purchase a house within my means and that I would be responsible for the mortgage. He became excited and said, "We've always wanted a house together. I would like to be a part of it, and we need to come back together." This should have been a red flag.

I had no doubt at the time he was serious, and it sounded good to me. We further discussed the plans and began house hunting until we found the ideal home. The house was situated in a quiet cul-de-sac. The lawns were well-kept and beautifully landscaped. It was the very place I wanted. It was a 2,400 square foot bi-level, four-bedroom home with two and a half baths and a family room. The backyard was very spacious and perfect for family outings. The house was more than I had envisioned. It was perfect for us. We were also surprised to find a home that suited both our taste and so quickly.

Dallas and I discussed the possibilities of the home being too large for our needs. However, we welcomed the idea of having a spacious home in case any of the children needed to come home temporarily. Also, if we came upon tough times, the house would be a place of security and would accommodate us all. We wrote down the contact information, and the rest is history. Not only were we homeowners, but my prayer was also answered, and we were together again as a couple.

Smooth Sailing Doesn't Mean God is in the Plan

The first few years in our new home were wonderful. We got along well, nurtured one another, and made God our priority. We bought new furniture, and Dallas even bought me a new car. He, along with my two nephews, made our family very comfortable in our beautiful new home.

I can't give a precise timeframe, but like deflating a balloon, our relationship began to spiral down until all the air was gone as things gradually fell apart and grew worse. The same past issues brought our marriage to irreconcilable differences and to an end again:

1) Dallas lost sight that self-stability and his family staying together depended 100% on him staying on his medication.

2) He was in and out of the hospital more than ever

3) Dallas slept 16-24 hours

4) Communication was broken and, at times, ceased

5) Blame and refusal to take ownership

6) Intimacy diminished

7) Secret phone calls and lies

8) God was no longer the heart of our relationship

Needless to say, my request and hope for a change didn't happen, nor did it last for long when any effort was made. I questioned the Lord, should I have been content with the house I envision with just the boys and me? Twelve rough years passed before I arranged to move out of the house. I chose to inform Dallas sooner than to spring it on him suddenly because schizophrenics don't handle major changes well.

Prayer Two

Talking to God throughout the day was natural for me. Whatever part of the house I found myself in, I communicated and connected with Him. One evening in 2007, I happened to be in the kitchen leaning on the counter drying a dish. My mind pondered on a passage of scripture in the Bible regarding the prophet Job and all he endured. In Job:6-22, God had a conversation with Satan that went like this: "Satan, where have you come from? Satan answered, from roaming throughout the earth… God asked, "Have you considered my servant Job… There is no one like him in…." Satan said to God, "Does Job fear God for nothing? If you take everything from Job, will he curse you to your face?" After God allowed Satan power over all Job had, except his life, Job lost his ten children, all his livestock, and most of his servants except four who survived to tell Job about the tragedies. Job was struck with boils from head to toe and he lost the respect and support of his wife. This was not the first time I meditated on the story of Job, but it was the only time my heart was full, and I requested of the Lord, "I desire for You to feel for me as you did Job. I would love for you to look at me as one of your servants that you can depend on and trust no matter what." Yes, those were my exact words. Not long after this prayer, the unthinkable began to happen.

First, I took custody of my son's three children, and after a year, I lost them to Child Protective Services. One of the worst pains in my life was on my morning commutes to work. I would lose concentration and break down into tears when I reflected on my four-year-old granddaughter's voice, who was now with a foster family. I still heard her cry, "Granny, why did you leave me? I love you." I begged God to please bring my grandchildren back to me. I mourned, "Lord, how can I tell Aaron I lost his children?"

Second, the vast majority of my life was spent working on my Master of Education. After teaching for Jefferson County School for over eleven years, I was accused of an incident irrelevant to my job. Hours were spent in court, week after week, month after month, and then turned into a year or more. I was demeaned, lied on, forced to listen to accusations hurled at me, not to speak of the misconceptions and misunderstandings regarding my case. I was prohibited from meetings that I had a right to attend. I endured racial comments written in the report. The CPS attorney and the Judge purposely switched court dates, deliberately failed to inform me, and when I showed up to court on the date we agreed upon, the Judge said I was a no show, and my case had already been heard. I observed court officials plot and verbally state that they were set out to ruin my career if I didn't stop fighting for my grandchildren, my rights, and justice for myself. I paid my first attorney only to have him fall prey to CPS lies.

I managed to hire a second attorney who was able to access the videos of what happened during both court hearing dates and revealed misrepresentation, committing fraud, etc. by the Judge and CPS Attorney. The adjudication process, in which my case was to go before a non-partial Judge, never happened. CPS findings against me were substantiated. Meanwhile, the Principal at Byck

Elementary was very supportive during the entire process, but in the end, the decision to let me go was out of her hands. The JCPS Superintendent knew my good-standing as a teacher yet feared, due to the nature of the charges, I was a liability to the school if any parent got wind of my case. The Board Superintendent presented me with two options, which were to resign or be fired. Rather than to have *terminated* on my record, I chose to resign.

For several years I endeavored to fight to retrieve my career; the funds just weren't there. Dallas was convinced the Judge wasn't going to give me back our grandchildren because of the time which had passed, so he refused to keep helping financially. Dallas didn't speak the same words as Job's wife; nonetheless, his actions illustrated the same attitude of Job's wife. Little by little, I lost everything that was of value to me: my home, marriage, grandchildren, career, and finances.

The Conclusion of the Matter

You'd be surprised by the encounters with God one can have over washing some dishes. Again, I am in the kitchen slumped over the counter, having another one of my quiet moments with God. I thought about all the drama and the devastating losses that had occurred so quickly in my life. As I thought of these things, that sweet familiar voice of the Holy Spirit spoke, *"Remember you said, God, I desire you to think of me as you did Job?"* It was as clear as water. I chuckled, dropped my head, sighed, and exclaimed, *"Lord have mercy."* The Spirit reminded me of my request for God to trust me as he did Job.

Be careful what you ask of God. In James, we are encouraged to examine our motives when requesting something of God and to ask "what is His will" before the request.

Trouble came and wouldn't stop. I didn't understand while I was going through, and although it was grossly painful, I pressed on. Am I sorry for what I ask of God? Absolutely not. I was sincere, well aware of what I asked, but I just didn't know the debt. God was probably thinking, *poor thing, she doesn't know what she is asking.* Once He revealed it to me, I had nothing but gratitude. Each petition was different, and the lessons learned were priceless. God allowed the testing and empowered me with immeasurable strength and perseverance. Because He is, Omnipotent (all-powerful), Omniscience (all-knowing), and Omnipresent (everywhere at one time), He knew what I was made of, and through these petitions, I found out. My faith soared to new levels, a new testimony was added to my journey, and it made me a stronger Bible teacher. Fortified faith comes with a trail of trials—be careful what you ask of God.

Chapter 13

Appearances are Deceiving

Have you ever made a decision about something or someone based on what you heard, seen, or thought only to find out it was the opposite? Assumptions are nothing more than one's personal preconceived, unsubstantiated opinions. Family, education, professional status, or religious affiliation does not make a person's perception or point of view legitimate or authentic. It is one thing to assume and ponder hearsay or obtained information, but it becomes problematic when inaccurate, questionable information is acted upon as being true. Many lives have been ruined due to misguided assumptions. It is the same as spreading malicious gossip. An assumption is symbolic to a supposition, inconsistencies evolved from (first, second, or third-hand information), assuming something is the case based on misinterpretations. How frequently are we readily receptive of what we perceive and hear before finding out the facts?

An assumption is a thing that is accepted as true or as certain to happen, without proof of which at times I stood guilty. I became attached to a man who had multiple external qualities, impeccable manners, intelligence, and spirituality, not realizing something was hidden. Things don't always appear as they are.

Dangers of Assumptions

1. Listening to assumptions press you to feel you owe an explanation, or you have to prove yourself.

2. Assumptions are overwhelming and lead to a frustrating spirit that can further disrupt a person's life.

3. When you doubt yourself, even though you are certain of the truth or what you believe, you become a victim of assumptions based on outside influences.

4. Listening to assumptions, one may presume it's not worth the risk of being misinterpreted and therefore are

reluctant to open up or share their troubles. People are going to believe what they want to believe anyway. While socializing with a friend at my kitchen table, a close acquaintance leaned over and kissed my chin. As his lips moved away from my face, he exclaimed, "Wow." Inquisitively, I asked, "What is it?" He replied, "Look at your face; you must have sensitive skin." I jumped out of my chair, ran to the bathroom, looked in the mirror, and saw a large red mark in the shape of a strawberry. My assumptions were, "What will the staff think? Will they think it's a passion mark that led to something further? My second instinct was to try and hide the mark versus letting it be revealed, and if someone inquired then, I would tell the truth. In your circle, you know who will assume the worse. Those closest to you can be callous and cold.

5. People, who hastily make assumptions toward others, rarely give forethought to the hardship which occurs to

an individual, a relationship, a colleague, a marriage, a company, a Pastor, or a congregation.

One of the reasons I delayed telling my story for fifteen years was due to the phobia of assumptions people would have as well as my own. Just because I assumed what people thought and how my story would be perceived didn't mean it was so. Precaution is wise before becoming engrossed in assumptions. Make sure the facts are straight before drawing conclusions.

Examples of Assumptions

➤ Your next-door neighbor is seen in a restaurant talking with someone of the opposite sex.

Assumption: He or she is being unfaithful or having an affair.

➤ You read in the newspaper that a CEO lost a position or company.

Assumption: A person must be involved in some type of embezzlement or corruption.

➤ A colleague has lost their home.

Assumption: The person must have mismanaged their funds or was negligent in paying

    the mortgage.

➤ A person is wandering in a park, lying on a public bench, or standing at a food bank.

Assumption: The person wants to be homeless, is lazy, does not want to work, can do

    better.

Biblical Assumptions

We are guilty of making preconceived assumptions of people's plight in life based on their past, current circumstances, culture, and demographics. Jesus was born in a barn with animals in the small town of Bethlehem. He was raised in a poor town called Nazareth, of which people thought very little. Jesus was a carpenter's son, and his mom was a poor virgin girl. It was difficult for the Jews, his own people, to believe Jesus was from God, was God in the flesh, and how could it ever be possible for Him to be a King, especially King of the Jews. *They claimed* an assumption, *"How can anything good come from Nazareth?*

In the second chapter of Joshua, we find a woman named Rahab, who ran a whore house. Later, through her knowledge of God, her household was saved, and she became part of the family of King David, whom our Lord and Savior Jesus was a direct descendant. **The assumption: That a person won't or can't change.**

A person suffers an unfortunate loss. For example, Job, a wealthy man, lived in a land called Uz. He lost all his material possessions, death took his children, and he lost the respect and support of his wife. **His buddies assumed Job's suffering was a result of sin.**

Jesus healed the man born blind, and the disciples assumed this man's parents and the man had sinned. Jewish leaders believed the same and treated him as such. **The assumption: Automatically, it is taken for granted the person did something wrong.** *"My dear brothers and sisters, understand this: Everyone should be quick to listen, slow to speak..." James 1:19 (CSB). "Don't jump to conclusions—there may be a perfectly good explanation for what you just saw." Proverbs 25:8 (MSG)*

During some dark times in my life, I experienced hurtful assumptions from misinformed, mean spirited folks, and here are some of their assumptions that were said to me and about me:

➤ "You married him for his money."

➤ "You had to know he was sick."

➤ "Didn't you see the signs?"

➤ "She's not happy."

- "She is holier than thou, walking around as if she has no problems."
- "She is the reason for the problems in their marriage."

Lastly, preconceived assumptions lead to people going to the extreme. During an intense time in my marriage, a young Deacon handed me a book by Charles R. Swindoll entitled Dropping Your Guard. The title of the book through me off. I analyzed and tried to figure out the motive behind my receiving it. The Deacon based my need for the contents of the book on the words of my spouse, who labeled me as the culprit in our relationship.

"For in the same way you judge others, you will be judged, and with the measure you use, it will be measured to you." Matthew 7:2. *"Don't be quick to tell a judge about something you saw. You will be embarrassed if someone else proves you wrong. If you want to tell your friends about your own problems, tell them. But don't discuss what someone told you in private. Whoever hears it will lose*

their respect for you and will never trust you again."

Proverbs 25:8-10 (ERV)

Don't allow assumptions to be a yoke. Having been a victim of this, my request of the Lord was to nudge me when I attempted to go in the direction of making assumptions. *"Treat others the same way you want them to treat you."* Luke 6:31 (NASB)

"When you're forming your opinions, do it carefully –go slow; hasty judgments are often followed by regretting –

that I know." –Anonymous

"This above all: To thine own self be true, and it must

follow, as the night the day,

Thou canst not then be false to any man." –Polonius

Chapter 14

Validating the Right Foundation

Have you forsaken your family in the time of a great need?

Matter has a variety of meanings, such as space of importance and significance, and whether something makes a difference. The core of validating the right foundation is to convey the significance of family, and how each member occupies space in the hearts and minds of one another with an understanding that life will bring about challenges and changes. Never forgetting about family is to function as a unit, no matter what the circumstances.

People who are allowed to occupy space and become partakers of our life, and the life of our children, can either build on the family foundation or will cause that foundation to crumble. I was a mother, Christian, protector, informant, teacher, and advocator for the welfare of all little people and duty-bound to advise children of any obstacles and hindrances that would place them in harm's way. Yet I asked myself, why couldn't I protect my own? My children mattered, and I would do anything to protect them. Nevertheless, I made a decision that was costly to the entire family. Why does family matter?

Family Began with God

Before the foundation of this world, family unity occupied a space in the mind of our Creator, God. Prior to our physical existence, we occupied a space in His mind. God foresaw humanity as a family unit with a man, wife, and children. The book of Genesis records God's creation of the first man, Adam, his wife Eve, and the special home He created for them in a garden called Eden. It was a place where God dwelled and met with the man Adam and Eve. God gave specific instructions to Adam and Eve to complete the family by reproducing children. Before the foundation of the world, God placed a significant value on the family unit, and it still exists today for God is absolute.

In the mind of an intentional Creator, the family was more than aforethought, a group of people occupying space and wearing the same name.

The expectancy of God is for the family structure to be built on love, devotion, trust, resilience, productivity, progressiveness, support, and sanctification, a nuclear family to last forever. The Bible is our scriptural blueprint for designing a vigorous family, the function of each family member, and how we are to care for one another.

"Anyone who doesn't provide for their relatives..." I Timothy 5:8 (NIV)

"Honor thy father and thy mother..." Exodus 20:12 (KJV)

"My son, hear the instruction of thy father..." Proverbs 1:8-9 (KJV)

"Train up a child..." Proverbs 22:6 (KJV)

"Children, obey your parents in the Lord: for this is right...Ephesians 6:1 (KJV)

And, ye fathers, provoke not your children to wrath...

Ephesians 6:4 (KJV)

"Wives, submit yourselves unto your own husbands, as

unto the Lord. Ephesians 5:22(KJV)

"Husbands, love your wives, and be not bitter against

them." Colossians 3:19

"Do not repay evil with evil and insult with insult..." I

Peter 3:9 (KJV)

Family is Our Foundation

A stern family is like a *"slab of concrete."* The solidarity, steadiness, and stability of the concrete foundation are based on the quality of the materials, and so it is with the family. Quality materials such as **truth and** knowledge, role modeling, respectability for humanity, etc., will determine family stability and 85-90% of the direction of that family. Exposures, disciplines, and functionality, extended family, optimism, right teaching, values, and morals, Biblical principles all contribute to the dynamics and convictions for a family's future. Beginning with a child's formative years, positive reinforcement and character building is essential and is an integral part of how the family journeys through this thing called life.

Family Influences What's of Value and How One Prioritizes Things in Life

The right influences and decision making are crucial for future aspirations and goals. Through family, one learns to prioritize the safety, emotional, mental, and physical well-being of the entire family. How individuals are to be viewed, respected, honored, and treated most likely spills over into our society. Ninety-nine percent of the time when you find disrespectful children, it started with their upbringing. If you don't think so, watch the news media. There are numerous domestic offenses, abuse, and homicides involving children.

The strength of a family isn't defined by the materialism of who drives a Porsche, is CEO, earned a

Ph.D., or lives in an upscale neighborhood or area. What does matters is whether the family is proportioned on lasting attributes of love, joy, peace, goodness, kindness, faithfulness, gentleness, and self-control.

Family is Inseparable in Body, Spirit, and Kindred Mind

God never asked us to hold to and believe anything that was not imperative to Him or that He did not set an excellent example. Since the beginning of time, God the Father, Jesus the Son, and the Holy Spirit are inseparable. Although they have separate distinctions and functions in purpose, the Trinity always operates as a family—One in body, spirit, and kindred mind regarding human destiny. Looking down through ceaseless generations with a desire to have fellowship with mankind, God sees my family and your family. The security and salvation of family are essential to God, the Father, Son, and the Holy Spirit. He extended unmerited favor (grace and mercy) that led all the way to the Cross of Calvary and caused a loving Father to momentarily turn His face away from the burdens of sin upon His Son's shoulder. *"I and the Father are one" John 10:30 (KJV) "He who has seen me has seen the Father..." John 14:9 (NKJV) "For I came down from heaven, not to do mine own will, but the will of him that sent me." John 6:38 (KJV)*

Family is God's Order

God is a God of order, a God of time, and of purpose. Everything He created functions as intended. The universe is set in order. The sun rises and sets, seasons come forth each on its time; leaves grow on trees, flowers bloom, and both die then start all over again in its season, and the animals and fowls of the air all have order and function. The human race made in the very image of God, the Father, and the Son is no different. God created man first, then woman, and they produced children in that order. It is safe to say that God placed man, the daddy, as the head of the family to rule by example, to take tender care of his wife and offspring.

Following the fall of Adam and Eve, and before God expelled them from the Garden of Eden, He explained to them that man was to be the head, and the woman was in subjection to her husband. Whether we like it or accept God's way, that's the way it is. God's written standards won't change.

Why the Presence of Fathers is Important to the Foundation of the Family

God's process of reproduction is complex but simple. During an ovulation period of a woman, male sperm can be fertilized inside her and produce a human offspring. Consequently, it is perfectly understood. What I want to emphasize is the fact that because of God's reproductive design, any male short of a physical defect can produce a child. The complexity comes when differentiating between a father, a male responsible for a baby birthed into the world, and a daddy.

Daddy is personable and is a feeling of close proximity. A daddy is a male father who is completely involved in every aspect of his child's life. A daddy is dependable, resourceful, comforts, teaches, and is a strong role model and gives sound advice with humility; his tone is authoritative, but not abusive. A daddy doesn't just dish out information; he explains and is not ashamed to succumb to a child's level to illustrate what he wants his child to learn. A daddy is willing to set goals, further his child's education, give the child his best self, and works hard to ensure the child's needs are fulfilled, and there is no lack. *"But I would have you know, that the head of every man is Christ; and the head of the woman is the man; and the head of Christ is God." I Corinthians 11:3 (KJV).*

I recall some, but very little experiences with my biological father. My father was short, fair-skinned, medium built, and good-looking. Other than hearing about it, the times I did lay eyes on my father, I remember he wore three-piece suits, a matching large brim hat, and shoes so shiny your face was reflected in the toe. He was an immaculate dresser. His two front teeth were gold plated, which illuminated his already contagious smile.

In the middle of one night, I needed to use the bathroom. On the way, I passed my mother's bedroom. Her door was opened enough for me to peek in and saw a pair of shiny brown shoes sitting neatly at the foot of her bed. Hanging on the bedpost was a suit coat. I knew it was him. Whenever my father visited, he didn't think it was important to say hello to his children before leaving our house.   The next morning after my father was gone, Mu-ah came to me and said, "Your father left you a quarter." Maybe a quarter had worth back in the day; however, it made me feel I wasn't valued. My siblings and I didn't seem to occupy too much space in the mind of my father, if any at all.

My mother died, and my older sister, Sandra, looked for my Father to share the news. Her exact words were, "I found your daddy." My heart leaped with excitement, which didn't last for long. She then said, "I told your father about Mu-ah's death and the funeral arrangements. He said, "They are not my children." What a blow to any child's heart/ego. I sat silently. He didn't attend the funeral, nor did we hear from him following the funeral. In fact, that was the last time I heard from my father. His place of residency was never made known to us. Throughout my whole life, I saw my father twice. Whether he was dead or alive, I couldn't tell you. He was never a *daddy* to me.

Family is Supportive

Hospitals and nursing homes are filled with people who have no one to call family. Children are left in foster homes, turned out on the streets for some reason or another with little or no support, families are experiencing more pressure, single-parent households are on the rise, jobs are scarce, and parents are working two and three jobs to make ends meet. Life challenges happen to people at different times in the form of politics, economy, sickness, death, finances, separation, and divorce. However, through it all, support needs to begin with the family.

I'm not saying there aren't times it becomes necessary to distant yourself from family or the circumstances. What I am saying is family is relational, and we need to be careful not to allow our ego to surface and interfere with meeting a need. In times of dark places and family controversy, it isn't a time to finger point, find fault or blame, which add fuel to the burning fire. Still, a time family should pull together versus becoming *self-oriented, self-absorbed*, or an *individualist*. Our focus should be on the matter of the problem, and not on victimizing. In times when one may prefer distancing self from family or an individual, there are creative ways of being supportive and doing your best to keep normalcy.

Appropriate communication is the key. Secretiveness and introversion are not always the best remedy. How will people know your pain and situation if you're not open? During trying times in my life, my family assumed I was a private person. They observed the external me and were clueless about my internal stance due to a lack of communication. My older sister was straightforward and told me I jumped out of the frying pan into the skillet. It was true. She didn't realize I was already crushed; I didn't need to hear those words. Supportive people:

➤ Carefully, choose their words

➤ Pray consistently

➤ Understand when silence is necessary and recognize it's their presence that counts

- Become a blanket of love, (prepare a dish, send a card, email, and a phone call, leave literature)
- Use wisdom about when to use scripture
- Are aware of the comfort of a hug; when leaving the person's presence, a hug will linger longer than a trail of words

A word of advice about hugging and touching from personal experience: I had a huge awakening about hugging. On my way to carry some items to the mortician for a dear sister in the Church, I received a phone call from her family member. Her sister was crying profusely while explaining her detachment from the deceased sister and of the pain and guilt she felt. I pulled on the side of the road to listen closely and console her as best I could. On the day of the funeral, this sister arrived at the funeral late, and so I didn't get to greet her along with the rest of the family. Following the recessional, our eyes locked, and I was excited to see her, so I reached to hug her. That was a huge mistake, one that practically knocked me off my feet. She drew back her hands as if she had touched a hot burner and let out a piercing squeal. *"Don't touch me!"* I was not expecting such a reaction. Quickly I regrouped by ignoring her reaction and to also avoid drawing more attention. Later, my daughter, who stood behind me at the time, asked me what was wrong with her.

If you are aware the person doesn't mind being touched, by all means do so. If you aren't sure, just to be safe, politely ask or extend a handshake.

Accept each family member as God's creation regardless of their character; they are worthy and entitled to the love and care you desire for yourself. As my Pastor put it, "We've got some crazy cousins, aunts, and uncles, but we are all family." For those who may not have the support of a family, there are two things to remember. First, support will not always come from your biological family; sometimes, an outsider will take the place of your family. Second, God will replace whatever you lack. He always has a ram in the thicket. Be assured, He will provide, and He'll send someone your way. *"When my father and mother forsake me, then the Lord will take me up." Psalms 27:10 "For a just man falleth seven times, and riseth up again: but the wicked shall fall into mischief." Proverbs 24:16 (KJV)*

"We who lived in the concentration camps can remember the men who walked through the huts comforting others, giving away their last piece of bread. Few in number, but they offered sufficient proof that everything can be taken from a man but one thing: the last of his freedom to choose one's attitude in any given circumstances, to choose one's own way."
--Frankl E. Victor

"Because of one's great love, one is courageous, from caring comes courage." --Tzu, Lao

Chapter 15

Schizophrenia

"Schizophrenia is a long-term mental disorder involving a breakdown in the relation between thought, emotion, and behavior leading to faulty perception, inappropriate actions and feelings. It is withdrawal from reality and personal relationships into fantasy, delusion, and a sense of mental fragmentation." Chronic Paranoid *Schizophrenia – "Is a subtype of schizophrenia in which the person has delusions (false beliefs) that a person or some individuals are plotting against them or members of their family."* (What is Schizophrenia? www.rtor.org)

Schizophrenia's unpredictability is mind-boggling, scary, and hard to withstand. The media reports horrific incidents, and various articles are written about instances of schizophrenics having committed heinous acts of violence. I can't claim to be an expert on schizophrenia; however, I can share my intimidations from personal experience. I married into a mental illness that happened to be chronic paranoid schizophrenia (CPS). If I were to cope with Dallas's illness, I couldn't afford to crowd my mind with reports of the media, nor could I feed off the experience others had with CPS or any other mental impairment. I had to individualize my husband's case.

Periodically, I was hopeful the illness would get better or that my husband would grow to maturity to better handle the illness. There were times when I felt hopeful that healing was taking place, but it was short-lived. Schizophrenia confounded my husband's doctors as we spent numerous times in his office exchanging information regarding which medications would calm unexplained behaviors. Upon finding out my husband was chronically ill, I made it a priority to learn all I could of its history, the likes/dislikes of schizophrenics, and what were the triggers.

CPS presented many teachable moments for him and me. My husband spent a year in the United States Army. For someone who had never been in active combat, my husband often went there in his mind. He had an outburst of screams so loud you would have thought the acoustics were in our home. He talked and answered himself. When passing me, it was like a swift, cool breeze, and strangely his eyes were set in a totally different direction from me. Somehow, we managed not to collide. At times I wondered if he consciously knew I was in the room. I observed him go from extreme emotional highs to extreme lows.

Perilous Inclinations

My husband went through periods of agitation, extreme obsessions with the family being in danger, especially when admitted to the hospital. When he called, his frantic voice would say things like, "Brenda, don't come up here, it's too dangerous. I tell you they're trying to poison or kill me. Stay home where it's safe. The whole family is in danger." The longer he was off his medication, the more psychotic and irrationally tuned into God he became. He straddled the bed or laid on the floor like a corpse with his arms stretched out, hands balled in fists, and in a catatonic state for hours. His eyes were fixated on the ceiling while comparing his sufferings to the crucifixion of Jesus. He believed God gave him spiritual revelations and powers that only he had the authority to interpret, and having these abilities strongly connected his spirit with God. The visions revealed to him were his reality. Many times, I was thankful he didn't translate the visions into action.

Graphic hallucinations, days, weeks, and months of depression, isolation, weight loss, dehydration, and unspoken words were his daily predicaments. Another one of the most frightening things he did was when he drove. More often than not, my husband took a notion to get on the highway while caught up in a trance or mental fog. In his early fifties, he began to drive less. Consciously, I believe he realized the distractions were critical, and he finally said, "I don't think I'll ever get on the road again."

Several times I recall my husband say, "I just want to live a normal life." Mental illness is real and definitely not a figment of one's imagination. The person dealing with the illness is in a different world with little boundaries because he or she is not in control of their mind. It's hard to have or keep a positive outlook on life if your mind is sick. I learned the various implications of what intensified Dallas's mental state, and what made it tolerable for me and him to be able to function together.

Quite often, in a typical discussion with my husband, he would say, "You never want to listen. A man has to make his own decisions." To which I replied, "Yes, it's true to a certain extent. Nonetheless, when a married man's decisions affect everyone in the household in a negative way, and if the decisions are reckless with intentions of gaining self-gratification, it becomes wrong, and the entire family suffers." Any response opposite of what Dallas wanted to hear ended the conversation. Explaining the difference between healthy decisions and making decisions leading to family disruption was like explaining to a child the need to remain on the sidewalk and why it's dangerous to ride a bike in the street. Unlike the normal mind, schizophrenics sometimes take years to learn from their mistakes, if ever.

"Habits are patterns of behavior that are regularly repeated and often occur without any conscious thought. A habit is an activity that has been commenced by a person and then is done regularly or repeatedly, quite often as an automatic process, and is found challenging to stop. When someone has this habitual behavior, they may not realize they are actually doing it. This is because it is a routine in their life that has become a subconscious activity." (What

the Bible Says About Breaking Habits.

www.bridgetothebible.com)

It's complicated enough to maintain a healthy mind, so it must be exhausting when the Devil plays games while your thoughts are discombobulated. *"Then Jesus asked him, "What is your name?" "My name is Legion," he replied, "for we are many." Mark 5:9 (NIV).* My husband had three strikes against him: compounding troubles, schizophrenia, and the Devil. All of this reaped havoc on his confused state and worked overtime on his mind, which caused him to look for a scapegoat for his shortcomings. He blamed anything and anyone for his fragile condition, and the fact remained he was his own worst enemy. He was like a grenade with a detached pen that was ready to explode.

Unfortunately, Dallas refused to take advantage of his support system (medication, group therapy, and mental health appointments), all of which would control some of the manic behaviors of schizophrenia. He functioned well, had more control and prolonged stability when he took the medication, remained in the Word and in fellowship with productive people. Quite the opposite was when he no longer prayed in a rational mind, detached himself from the spiritual, and alienated himself from life period. Dark times call for drastic measures. Schizophrenia drove me to fasting and to my knees many days and nights, losing myself in singing the *HELL OUT* of my house and declaring these liberating words, "Satan, you have no power over me."

"Resist the devil and he will flee from you." James *4:7 (KJV). "Be alert and of sober mind. Your enemy the devil prowls around like a roaring lion looking for someone to devour. Resist him, standing firm in the faith..." I Peter 5:8-9 (NIV). "Let us not become weary in doing good...at the proper time we will reap a harvest if we do not give up." Galatians 6:9 (NIV)*

Would Anything Relieve Us of this Plight?

A farmer patiently cultivates the soil, plants the seeds, and is confident that with rain and sunlight, he will produce a harvest. As with the farmer, when we've done our best, God will step in and lift us above our infirmities. Regardless of our past or current situation, we look forward to a spiritual harvest.

➤ Harvest of joy

➤ Harvest of kindness

➤ Harvest of forgiveness

➤ Harvest of genuine love

➤ Harvest of peace

➤ Harvest of hope

➤ Harvest of faith

➤ Harvest of eternity

"The battle is not mine; it is the Lord's," is a scripture reminding me that the fight wasn't with my husband. If I were to ever succeed in this warfare, to resist the attacks on our family, I had to make a daily effort to use my spiritual tools. An external façade with time fades leaving one with pretense and bewilderment of the inner persona, and always finding oneself to be the opposite of what one professes to be.

"Facade"

External — Living My Best Life

Internal — Thirsty-Dissatisfied-Disoriented

External — Fame, Popularity, Loved

Internal — Unvalued and Incompatible

External — Smiling

Internal — Crying out-Worthless-Despondent-Sadness

External — Self-Assured

Internal — Inadequate and Deficient

The above poem resonates with our struggle. Although my smiles and laughter were genuine, internally I was hurting. The poem also depicts my husband's struggle between two forces. Proximity is the core of knowing somewhat how one feels without a saying a word. Dallas implicated the hurt of being misunderstood, abandoned by his biological family, and beneath the perplexity. I believe sometimes Dallas felt abandon by God. Schizophrenia took my husband to places that if he were in his right mind, he would have never entertained. He concluded that the demands to leave this world would resolve the longevity of mental suffering. Dallas showed he was tired of the mental mask, and he didn't like the man brewing within. He wasn't pleased with the man he had become.

I recall a time when conscientious instincts prodded me to check on Dallas since he hadn't been seen in a while. Having traveled this route over and over, I still found myself on pins and needles not knowing what to expect. Reluctantly and slowly I walked up the steps towards Dallas's apartment, then I saw his apartment door was open. My first thoughts were how long had the door been open? I stepped inside the apartment door and heard the

TV buzzing. I eased down the hallway and saw no sign of Dallas. Then I walked back up the hallway peering in each room, this time I entered the bedroom. It was there I found him sitting in the open closet. His frail body frame looked to weigh no more than 98 pounds. Between his legs was a plastic gallon jug half-filled with water. This was a sure sign he was on another one of his fast. His pants were soaked with urine. Immediately I called an ambulance, and Dallas was transported to the hospital.

There were many times my husband and I discussed mixing drugs with alcohol, and so he was aware of the complications. After the ambulance left, it gave me more time to concentrate on what Dallas had been doing in the apartment. Shockingly, around the walls were gallon jugs of vodka, whiskey, bourbon, cognac, gin, and wine. I can't honestly claim all his reasons for drinking, but one thing I was certain, the alcohol was meant to drown out the voices in his head. I knew I didn't want him to come home to any of this, so I got rid of it all before leaving the apartment. A delusional mind combined with drinking would send my husband further down a path of self-destruction. To this day, Dallas says, "I would have been an alcoholic had it not been for my wife." God used me as a vessel at the right time.

His Way of Escape

To say Dallas was miserable is an understatement. He wanted out of that schizophrenic life by any means necessary. Schizophrenia misguided him to use excessive and unwarranted measures to find a way out and to put an end to what he felt was hopeless.

I directed the choir during a Sunday evening program. Following the service, my Pastor pulled me aside, and told me Dallas tried to hurt himself. Over the years of dealing with the illness, acting in fast mode was my normal. I could be scared, upset, and at the same time calm and in control. After making sure my children were in good care, I headed for the hospital. The doctor said Dallas tried to stab himself in the heart. By grace, he missed his heart and punctured the pericardium, which is the sac-like tissue surrounding the heart. After a week in intensive care and a thirty-day stay in the hospital, he was discharged with minor respiratory problems. During his suicidal attempt, **God spared him the first time.**

After learning about another one of my husband's disappearances, I visited his apartment. While knocking on the apartment door, I heard a sound like an animal pawing and scratching from within. With each knock, the sound became louder. I called my husband's name, but there was no response. Instead, there was a rattling and fumbling of the doorknob, so I yelled for Dallas to open the door. Ten minutes had gone by, and he finally got a grip on the knob, so I gave it a little push and slowly the door opened. There was Dallas stumbling and falling to the floor. The look on his face showed he was glad to see somebody. I talked to keep him coherent.

A number of open pill bottles were spread over the entire countertop, along with a large football-shaped tray filled with pills. Immediately I called 911. Dallas was taken to the hospital, and his stomach was pumped. **God spared him a second time.**

Dallas filled the bathtub with water and submerged his head beneath the water. I don't know how many times he attempted, but he didn't succeed. **God spared him a third time.**

When Dallas was found in New York walking the streets with no shoes, he was on a mission. He later confessed his aim was to go there hoping something would happen to him on the streets of New York. **God spared Him a fourth time.**

"Oftentimes, people consider suicide because they're unable to find any reason to make living worthwhile. They think their problems are unsolvable, and they feel completely out-of-control. First and foremost, I believe that hopelessness is a serious spiritual problem rooted in lies and faulty thinking." (Why Do People Commit Suicide?_ www.hopeline.com/why-people-commit suicide? McAllister Dawson Network)

If things couldn't get worse, one evening Dallas came to the apartment in 80-90-degree weather wearing black leather attire with a depressing blank look over his face. Repeatedly he spoke on death and no longer wanting to live in this world. Honestly, I don't know if the Holy Spirit was leading me; I just know my patience was no longer tolerant of his suicidal talk and attempts. Anger took control over me, "Kill yourself then! Go on and kill yourself! Try to kill yourself as many times as you want! If it's not God's will, you are not going to die. You may cause harm to yourself by trying, but you're not going anywhere." Right or wrong, it didn't seem to matter; I couldn't retrieve my words. Dallas's countenance took on a darker color, and he gnashed his teeth. I wasn't sure what his next move would be, thank God he turned away and stormed out the patio door. Surely, he wasn't expecting to hear those words from my mouth. According to Dallas, he made five suicide attempts. I am aware of four attempts, not to mention the countless times he placed himself in harm's way where he could have died. Often times my harshness with Dallas was generated from concern and was an attempt to snap him back into reality. "Do you not understand you are still here? God must have a purpose for you," I sometimes explained.

What to Do When Enough is Enough

I saw Dallas mentally exhausted from living in a body he felt he could not control. I held to the fact that God was able. It was possible for Dallas to maintain some stability with help, but it wasn't happening. Mentally not knowing what else could be done other than what we had tried to do over the years was frustrating. Listening to me was taboo, and Dallas convinced himself that communication of any kind from me was meant for evil, to tear down, and to further drive him to a fork in the road. He blamed his sickness on the medications and my constantly admitting him to the hospital for no apparent reason. Over the years, countless hours were spent at the Mental Inquest Warrant Office. My husband had been to court so many times that MIW Staff, Judges, and State Guardianship Case Workers all recognized his name, and they were frighten of him because of his overpowering demeanor, tone, gestures, and the discovery of immense MIW files. Even his attorney became annoyed as well. They simply did not know what to do or how to help him.

Neither did I, so I cried out to the Lord to take Dallas home. If for no other reason, there would be no worry for consistent mental relapses worsening the condition. Dallas was not an exception. I observed most mentally unstable people tend to turn against those closest to them. They think family and friends are the enemies and those with "*healthy minds*" are the sick ones.

My personal encounters with schizophrenia taught me the following essentials to healing and coping with the disease of my husband.

1. Acknowledgment (Admitting your loved one suffers from a debilitating disease)

2. Acceptance (Own it and willingness to take responsibility)

3. Education (Understanding the illness, how it works on the mind, body, and spirit, etc.)

4. Individualization (Not all mentally ill people are the same. What works for one may not work for another)

5. Counseling (Collectively and individually seek help and resources)

6. Know when to be gentle and when to use tough love (Find coping mechanisms)

7. Prayerful (Being specific with God and believing nothing is "too hard and impossible with God")

Out of the seven points listed above, education is an opportunity to get acquainted with what you are dealing with and to stay in touch with people who are qualified to help you through. Educated also enables you to retain the symptoms, triggers, and cease to personalize, internalize, become outraged with the behavioral mood swings, and not be easily discouraged by schizophrenia's rejections.

"Saying, Touch not mine anointed, and do my prophets no harm." Psalms 105:15 (KJV). This passage of scripture is powerful. I knew God loved my husband, I knew the debt of the illness and the destruction done to Dallas; however, I was toughened by the fact He watched over our children and me. Schizophrenia didn't take me out or rob me of my sanity because I relied totally on God to protect me from that which was invisible.

Chapter 16

27 Years Married—10 Years Divorced, But Was I?

Married and alone is a lonely place to be.

Dallas, schizophrenia, and I endured twenty-seven years of marriage consisting of withstanding years of peaks, valleys, and numerous separations. The longest consecutive time we were in the same house was over a period of twelve years before I, without a doubt, knew our marriage had come to an end, and I moved out of the home into an apartment. After I filed for the divorce, there was a sense of freedom. I was willing to have a long-distance friendship, for I didn't see Dallas as an enemy. Be that as it may, the connections I once had with him were over, so I thought.

There were a few years of aloofness before I found out my youngest, Knijel, had taken guardianship for her daddy. The arrangement appeared to work until my daughter called and informed me Dallas was sick. She and I talked through the familiar signs of the illness and the medication. I reminded her of my decision to not involve myself with Dallas, his illness, or any help because I was over and done with him. Knijel was frustrated and added, "I know Momma, but you will be helping me."   My daughter was reenacting the "Good Samaritan," and so how could I, as her mother, refuse my child's cry for help and to make her endeavors as easy as possible. Against my better judgment, I committed myself to the cumbersome task. The shadow of schizophrenia was still moving in my direction, or I was moving in it, only it was in a new time, a new place, and in a new phase of my life.

Knijel's work schedule prevented her from checking in with Dallas at night and especially during the times he was off his medications.   She needed me to go check on him and my grandchildren. Dallas's residency with our daughter didn't last for long. Eventually, he was placed back in the hands of the State Guardianship, and of course, there was a repeat of the past with inefficient and incompetent caseworkers, their attitudes, and inattentiveness to his needs. Dallas moved to one home care after another with a combination of in-house problems such as bed bugs, late meals, unattractive rooms, and insufficient seating for state guardians and medical consultants. They had to sit on the floor during his assessment. You would think at least one of these guardians or medical consultants would have reported the situation or reprimanded the caretaker, but it never happened. Finally, over a period of time and getting the attention of a passionate caseworker, Dallas's request to move was granted. Wouldn't you know it, the first words from his mouth was to relocate to my apartment complex.

The irony was with all the problems he claimed to have with me, he wanted to be near me. Politely I advised against the idea. Anyway, Dallas moved in a condominium up the street from me, and I am talking five minutes tops within walking distance and two minutes in a car. Lord, will I ever get away from him? The older in age he became, schizophrenia made it difficult for Dallas to manage and maintain living quarters in any residence. Our children, me, and infrequently some of our older grandchildren were involved in checking on Dallas. We gave him verbal reminders to take his shot, calling 911 for wellness checks, which did not always work in our favor, among other essentials for his care. When necessary, we resorted to filing a Mental Inquest Warrant.

Throughout previous years, Psychologist and Mental Hygienists made me aware that Dallas's inconsistencies with meds and frequent relapses would one day interfere with him returning to his normal self. They were right. Erratic behaviors became more bizarre. Instead of being hospitalized once or twice a year, he was hospitalized three to five times a year. The minimum stay for a patient on the VA Psychic Ward was two weeks at the most. With each admission, normal functioning of his mind required changes in meds (higher dosages) to bring him back to some sense of reality. Discharges from the hospital were challenging when I knew Dallas wasn't ready to come back into society. Weeks in the hospital were prolonged into months by pleading with the VA Mental Health Consultant, his Doctor, VA Court Administrators, and a Judge.

Sometimes this strategy didn't work because even the hospital staff became frustrated, and he was sent home regardless of his mental state. Occasionally as soon as I laid eyes on him, I knew. His eyes were as wide as a fifty-cent coin, glassy, and watery. He was fidgety, hallucinating, and his judgment was cloudy as if he had no medication in his system. He slept through an entire day and sometimes 48 hours, only getting up to use the bathroom, which was not often. Within a day or a week, he was readmitted to the hospital. He was out-of-control and more defensive than ever, and ranting the medication caused his sickness.

Clearly, he wasn't mentally ready for early discharge or to return to his living quarters without supervision. Again, Caseworkers left him non-medicated for months and in deplorable conditions. I couldn't count the number of times we reported negligence to the state. After years of practice and experience, my brain was imbedded with the mental protocol of Dallas's routine, condition, and behavioral patterns. In May of 2016, Dallas's condition caused him to be "high risk" as he suffered from severe dehydration and just a thread from slight kidney failure. His surroundings were that of a hoarder. Repetition of court appearances and mental inquest warrants were unavoidable.

Dallas had burnt so many bridges even the State Guardianship grew tired. His vulgarity, rude gestures, unpredictability, and untidy hygiene caused disdained for Dallas and court officials, including certain Judges who weren't courteous to him. As a matter of fact, his Attorney demonstrated more intimidation than professionalism in representing him until it became disturbing. I emailed his Attorney opposing his negligence for Dallas during representation which read: "*Attorney M, you fight hard to protect his assets and finances, but fail to represent him as being an ill person, incompetent and with a long-term condition which is not always controlled through medicating or just because of what people think the person should be doing or acting. Today in court, I hope you will see Dallas as a human with needs and fight for him to live in a clean/safe environment.*" I further explained, Dallas was not always that man they were accustomed to seeing. He was quite the opposite. I was frustrated with the unprofessionalism and reminded his Attorney and State Guardianship of their responsibility to protect despite his illness and actions. Needless to say, they remained nonchalant. Time was of the essence and so I moved to speak to their superiors. Prior to the court hearing, I submitted documentation of Dallas's mental status and surroundings to the Head of Guardianship in Frankfort, to the Louisville Guardianship Supervisor, and to the Officiating Judge and his Attorney.

Fred R. Barnard said, "*A picture is worth a thousand words*." I submitted photos that told the story, which showed garbage piled up from the bedroom to the living room and to the kitchen. Instead of sheets, every inch of his mattress was covered with restaurant food bags, containers, condiments, napkins, open food cans, and whatever he had eaten remained on his bed. The toilet was filled with feces and had been stopped up for months. Obviously, the Landlord wasn't on her job. Shamefully the situation continued. When Dallas would open his door, our children and grandchildren occasionally did what they could to help.

I was in no shape to help because my physical body drastically changed. One day I woke up and my right foot was turned outward. The more I tried turning my foot to its normal position, it was not happening. As time went on, I began to have back pain, which felt like the tip of a knife was stuck in the middle of my lower back. I walked with a limp accompanied by excruciating pain that drove me to tears. A crutch enabled me to have minimum balance, to hold up my torso, and to support my wobbly legs. My leisure walk reverted to the steps of a toddler. After many MRI's and CAT scans, I was diagnosed with spondylolisthesis (slippage of the spine). I had two at L4 and L5, with a herniated disc, compressed nerves, and arthritis in my lower back.

Due to chronic pain levels exceeding ten, my blood pressure consistently skyrocketed and maintained high levels, which caused me to be admitted to the hospital three times. One Sunday morning in 2014, I was feeling tired and weak, nothing out of the norm since I suffered from fibromyalgia. I got dressed and went to worship, taught a Bible class, and it was then I noticed something peculiar. A child said to me, "Sister Brenda, that's not my name." I looked at this child and couldn't recall his name. Following worship, a couple of the members and I set in the pews talking, but I couldn't get out or finish what I was trying to say. Now, knowing something was obviously off, I told one of the sisters something was wrong with me. I left worship and went to a friend's apartment because I didn't want to go home and concentrate on my pain. The problem worsened. My friend had to help me complete my thoughts.

I left her apartment, went home, and went to sleep. Around 10:30 pm, I woke up and took my BP, which read 199/104. At the time, I was unable to reach my daughters.

So, I drove to my friend's home, and her son took me to the hospital. I met my daughter in the Emergency Room. Triage took my vitals, and my BP reading was 238/124. I was admitted on a Sunday night and remained in the hospital through Christmas week. The following Wednesday, I was diagnosed with (TIA), a mini-stroke, and loss of self-expressive language and blood flow to the brain. On Friday, I was as good as new, praise God. I made it through without any side effects from the stroke.

There was still an existing problem. The doctor's exact words to me were, "The TIA is before the big one." Surgery was no longer optional, and my body couldn't continue to combat the pain. Either I have surgery, or I take a huge risk in having a massive stroke. The thought of back surgery was frightening; I stayed in prayer. My spinal surgery was set for September 26, 2014, at 2:30 p.m. Wanting any amount of pain relief, on the morning of the surgery, I anxiously awaited the Anesthesiologist to walk in the room. A five-hour surgery turned into eight hours. Although the spinal fusion was a success, not all went as planned. My first week in rehab, infection set in, and I went back to the hospital for a second surgery. I looked forward to being pain-free, getting stronger, and above all, walking. Months went by, and that wasn't the case. The anniversary of my surgery, September 26, 2015, came and went, but there was still no pain relief, and neither was I walking.

The pain in my legs and thighs were unbearable. The only temporary relief and help for bearing with it was the use of a walker and wheelchair. My social life declined, my independence was at an all-time low, driving privileges ceased. It was a chore and painful to get myself out of bed and take care of my hygiene. There were days I balled up like an embryo with flowing tears, and the pain at night refused to let me sleep. In the midst of it all, I was bothered that I could no longer engage in my normal busy routine. I had thoughts of all I had been through, and now this. I prayed for God to give me some relief and give me back the use of my legs. Perhaps I needed to slow down, and had I not slowed down, would I have taken the time to write and complete this book? My answers came in this form, and I held on to it. All I knew was:

➢ God is a Promise Keeper; He met all my needs.

➢ He performs miracles, and I trusted Him to get me through.

➢ His infinite wisdom and timing never ceased to amaze me.

➢ Physically afflicted, I still had to worship, serve, and be an example of a Christian.

➢ God is worthy of all my praise, even under unpleasant circumstances.

➢ This journey was an additional testimony.

Physically Unable but Used as a Vessel to Help Dallas

Even though I went through a valley of physical issues and ended up in a wheelchair, I was still compelled to help Dallas. During the time I was dealing with physical issues, the most I could do was to ask the kids to check on him. Dallas remained in the mental and deplorable state for an entire year before I was able to return to the Mental Inquest Court. Throughout the entire hearing, I dealt with a Judge who acted with pure sarcasm. She had the audacity to recommend me to take out a Mental Inquest Warrant when she was the contacting Judge who denied the first inquest, and I didn't refrain from letting her know it as well.

After filing paperwork twice before the Judge signed off when the court papers were finalized, I started the procedures to have Dallas transferred from his Condo to the VA Hospital. While he was admitted, I worked on finding a safe place for him to reside. This was another challenge. No one would accept him because of the mental diagnoses or because of his past/current medical behavior records. I was thankful I could still drive again, and I had the support a Sister in Christ and dear friend, Darlene Bibb, who helped me get my wheelchair in and out of the car. She also so gracefully pushed me in the wheelchair so I could take care of all the necessary business for preparing for Dallas to have a place of residency following discharge from the hospital. When the final arrangements were made, Dallas was accepted as a resident in an assisted living facility. I had one more thing to take care of. I went to the VA hospital and shared with him in detail what was going to take place, papers for him to sign, and showed him pictures of his new home. Most importantly, I said to him, the Lord said to me, this is the last time to help him. I told him if he got put out of this place, I would no longer be involved in finding him another home again.

Dallas moved to Oxmoor Lodge Assisted Living, a beautiful, spiritual, and peaceful place. He had nothing to do but move in and enjoy. Three meals a day served on china dishes plus snacks were available 24 hours a day. He had access to housekeeping, transportation, the option of in-house laundry, or to pay for personal laundry care. There were daily entertainment and tangible activities, holiday celebrations, field trips, family days, religious activities, worship services, security, and a host of other amenities. The facility was beautiful; most importantly, since going in public and especially to the doctors was difficult for Dallas, he also had the privileged and was entitled to have an incoming Nurse Practitioner to administer his monthly shot. This would cut down on him going long periods without medication in his body. This was Dallas's last hope. It was court-ordered permanently, and he could no longer live in unsupervised living arrangements because no other place in Louisville would accept him long term. Doctors were pushing for him to be sent out-of-town to the closest VA facility, which was in Cincinnati or Tennessee, and none of us wanted that to happen. I was beyond ecstatic, the people accepted Dallas and were willing to work with him, and we felt our worries were over. Several months into his new home, Dallas was on the verge of eviction for noncompliance. If his lease were terminated, where would he go? My plea was, "Lord, if it's Your will, take him home. I'd rather see him go home with you than for him to be sent out-of-town away from family or back on the streets--yet I know, Lord, it's not my call."

I vented my feelings to my daughter, Knijel, who responded, "Momma, I am not ready for daddy to die." Not trying to persuade her my way but wanting her to understand my perspective of the situation with Dallas, I explained that my request was no different than when we pray for God to take home a person who is suffering in their last stage of cancer. I shared with her about a relevant situation of the recent death of a church member and friend, Kate. My friend suffered immensely from multiple illnesses and had gone through major surgeries, even amputation of one limb. I told Knijel how various times my friend had not healed from one operation before scheduled for a different surgery. I watched her cringe and scream as her pain seemed endless. Long story short, Kate was being prepped for her third heart surgery. She was shouting out from the pain. I dropped my head, "Lord, how much more pain can a person take." Shortly, Kate passed from this life. I was saddened by the news, not for long because I found peace knowing God understood. He knew my existing physical condition and the difficulty of visiting and taking care of my friend. It is my belief God will end the suffering for both the ill person and the caregiver as well.

As a result of my relationship with God, I had no fear of judgment to speak with Him on that level, and He knew the intent of my heart. On the contrary, I respected God as the Righteous Judge. He feels deeply when we mourn, and most imperative regardless of my feelings, I was fully aware He doesn't base His decisions according to our emotions. Our prayers have to be in accordance with His perfect will, purpose, and timing. I was blessed to be able to pour my heart out to Him.

Things were heating up at the assisted living facility. Dallas was all over the place. He was invading the space of residents, preachy, carrying a stench from bad hygiene, and staff, and some of the tenants were in an uproar and petitioned for him to leave the premises. In the meantime, Dallas swore to me, "Brenda, I took a shower. I'm keeping my voice down. I'm not talking loudly. I go to my room to calm myself down. I'm not bothering anybody."

Child-like confessions coming from Dallas were *milestones.* I believed him to be sincere and that Dallas desired to maintain control. I resorted back to his character the way I used to know him, when he was rational, had immaculate hygiene, poised and respectable. If he could just understand medication was an integral part of his wellness. He was evicted from Oxmoor Lodge and now lives with my younger daughter, Knijel.

Marriage to Dallas Was a Dilemma

My journey with schizophrenia has been long and tedious. This book is only a small portion of my walk in the shadow of my husband's illness. In moments of solitude, I pondered if I had seen actions that would have exposed his illness, perhaps I wouldn't have married him. I questioned did I make a mistake, or was my marriage to Dallas supposed to take place for a higher purpose? During my times of reflection and searching, Job came to mind when he questioned God about his sufferings. God never revealed to Job an answer.

Another time I pressed God for an answer, I was directed to the Prophet Hosea. I immersed myself in this passage about Hosea found in the first chapter. God instructed Hosea to go outside his spiritual realm/tradition to marry a promiscuous woman, a prostitute, a woman outside of Jewish customs by the name of Gomer. As odd and strange as the command was to Hosea, God had an intentional purpose far beyond Hosea's comprehension and it was to teach Israel and bring them back into His loving arms. Was God consoling me, letting me know it's okay, it was His will, or was I convincing myself that marrying Dallas and bringing him into my children's life was not my own mistake?

I want to believe I listened and followed God's guidance in making the decision. (Did I make a mistake? What did I miss? Did I overlook the signs? Was Dallas supposed to be a temporary part of my earthly journey? Was my marriage a divine calling for a season? Was I a vessel to be used to help Dallas? It remains a dilemma. All I can do is cherish the lessons walking in the shadow of a schizophrenic has taught me.

1. I am a vessel to be used. God handpicks His children for a task at an appointed time. There are people in this world who God wants to bring to the foot of the cross and may want to use us to accomplish His will. In doing so, one may have to endure longsuffering and persecution.

2. Acceptance of God's will bring peace in the midst of the struggle. I understand the significance of *"...My grace is sufficient..." II Corinthians 12:9 (NIV)*

3. People won't always understand why you do what you do and will lean toward human perspectives.
   "The LORD does not look at the things people look at. People look at the outward appearance, but the LORD looks at the heart." I Samuel 16:7 (NIV).

4. God will work the bad out for our good.

Some Biblical examples are:

➤ Jesus was destined to die, but lack of understanding of the Spiritual Kingdom and Jesus' deity, His own rebelled against Him and aided His crucifixion.

➤ Jesus couldn't perform miracles in his hometown (Nazareth), due to unbelief.

➤ On the day of Pentecost, Jews made accusations of the Apostles because of their limited knowledge and understanding of the Holy Spirit's Power.

➤ Prophet Daniel was thrown into the lion's den due to the King Nebuchadnezzar refusing to recognize Daniel only prayed and remained true to his God.

➤ Babylonians threw Shadrack, Meshach, and Abednego into a fiery furnace because they refused to eat King Nebuchadnezzar's food.

➤ Joseph, an interpreter of dreams, was sold to an Egyptian caravan because of his brother's hatred.

➤ Stephen was rejected and the first Christian to be murdered for his faith and preaching the truth about Jesus.

God accomplishes His will through incomprehensible ways and through people of whom we feel may not fit the profile. God qualifies whom He chooses and equips them with all the essentials to complete the task. He knows who can be trusted with His plan despite the consequences, obstacles, and opponents, so He alone gets the glory. *God graciously invites people who believe in Him to be a part of His plan."* *www.whychristmas.com.*

I confessed my soul to God, Lord, if the decision to marry Dallas was wrong, forgive me. If my marriage was your providential plan, I accept my plight and will gladly tell my story. I felt relieved knowing God looks at the heart.

My children and I were survivors of the enormous hurdles of chronic paranoid schizophrenia. A relationship with Christ nurtured me, and as a result, I could push past the pain, treat Dallas with respect, and do right by him. As a former teacher, holding an eight-hour job, taking care of a family, dealing with schizophrenia, endured multiple surgeries, and engaged in the mission of the Church, God gave me immeasurable *stamina*. I refused to allow schizophrenia or my physical disabilities to manage or master me. When God is the center of your life, He controls your mind, body, and spirit. *"He maketh my feet like hinds' feet, and setteth me upon my high places."* *Psalms 18:33 (KJV)*

Grace enabled me to see the goodness of the Lord above the continual darkness in my circumstances, and I was assured God was pleased with my endeavors. My children and I saw Dallas through spiritual eyes. Jesus, while we're on this journey, lend us Your eyes. *"I had fainted, unless I had believed to see the goodness of*

the LORD in the land of the living." Psalms 27:13 (KJV)

Chapter 17

The Main Thing is to Love One Another

Do you lack empathy for differences? Mental illness is not new. It's been around for ceaseless ages. What is new is how the mentally impaired have been dealt with, scientific understandings of the brain changes, the causes, and a vast amount of medications to relieve the psychosis of the brain. *"You can't just magically think your way out of a mental illness, whether it's mild or severe. This idea is pervasive-and damaging because it creates unreasonable expectations for the person who is suffering from the illness." You Can Snap Out of Mental Health Problems, Nelson Friemer, MD.* I found you couldn't pray away a mental illness either.

Past Treatment of Mental Disorders

Earlier history and prevailing theory of psychopathology was the idea that mental illness or abnormal behaviors were a result of demonic possession, evil spirits, witchcraft, or an angry god. People exhibiting strange behaviors were misunderstood, treated cruelly, and various forms of treatment were used to release spirits from individuals. For example, exorcism—prayers conducted by a Priest or religious figures; trephination—a small hole was made in the individual's head to release spirits from the body of which most died; execution or imprisonment, and some were left to be homeless beggars.

Today there are Community Mental Health Centers across the nation, located in neighborhoods providing people with mental health services. Underfunded centers increased financially and are equipped with proficient and trained staffing.

In Biblical times, I believe the mentally ill were referred to as demon possessed. Saul, the first King, was said to be tormented with an evil spirit from the Lord. Nebuchadnezzar suffered from insanity for seven years.

Legion was a man with multiple unclean spirits. Mary Magdalene had seven demons, and other women were cured of evil spirits, etc. Jesus dealt with individuals of this magnitude and treated them no differently than the rest of the crowds of folks with issues. In fact, Jesus had nothing but compassion and intent to see them whole both spiritually and physically. In the cities of Tyre and Sidon, a woman asked Jesus to heal her daughter possessed by a demon.

We don't know all the scientific reasons for mental illness or why some lose their sanity. What we must agree on is the way we handle people who are shackled with the disease. There should be no respecter of persons. Jesus, during his three and a half years ministering, set the example for all humanity by extending love and compassion to those with bowed head, the forgotten, poverty-stricken, and the diseased, etc. Jesus went to the lowest geographical places, forbidden areas, and places others refused to go bringing awareness that all suffered from some kind of sickness or another due to no fault of their own and all were in need of healing. How often do we forget we are sinners saved by grace and that we should look at others in a different light? Some of us sin louder.

Our treatment of people based on personal perception and biases is horrifying. Why are some folks given special attention and treatment? Why do we place ourselves above others because of their physical and mental infirmities? Why do we isolate ourselves from the unknown versus having the heart to want to understand? Why is it we refuse to relate to the inflictions of others until it hits home? Why are the mentally ill in our society excluded? For example, a mental person enters the church doors, if they get in, and folks clam up and are ready to send them back to the street or call law enforcement. How many ushers rush to seat a mentally ill person in the church? Instead, these folks are approached with reservation, treated as though they're undeserving of a greeting, a smile, a handshake, or a welcome back. Normally the ill person drifts in and finds space on a back pew. God forbid the person sits down beside a believer. The first reaction is to grab personal belongings and almost sit in the lap of the person on the opposite side to avoid close proximity. Worship is hardly over before the hard looks, and the gossip begins. I've heard comments like, "Did you see him/her? Girl, he/she was acting weird and crazy. What is he/she doing here anyway? Wasn't that so-and-so's husband or wife? Did you smell them?" During fellowship dinners, the mentally ill are the last ones offered to eat. They sit over in a corner or are left standing on a wall. Reactions may not be intentional; nevertheless, it is inexcusable, and we need to be more conscientious. Last, the mentally ill are judged and viewed as trouble and handled as if they need to repent of their illness and the Lord's house is no place for them.

I am not aware of any hospital that excludes people and turns them away on the bases of who they are and their condition. The Church is a hospital in the midst of a fallen world, and everyone is compelled to come. Congregations should be filled with Blacks, Hispanics, Asians, Native Americans, Caucasians, liars, gossipers, prostitutes, pimps, drunks, mentally ill, homeless, disable, handicap, homosexuals, gang bangers, wayward teens, elderly, saved, and unsaved. No one should be rejected or ruled out. Conditions vary, undoubtedly all have one thing in common, sickness, a condition needing a physician and immediate attention. *"It is not the healthy who need a doctor, but the sick. I have not come to call the righteous, but sinners." Mark 2:17 (NIV).*

The mentally ill need the truth and a relationship with Jesus in hopes they too will make a difference in someone's life, and perhaps even another who has suffered from mental impairments. We never know what people are dealing with or what their state of mind is, and we make the mistake of focusing on the external. The Church is a place where folks should be made to feel accepted.

The Pettiness of Seasoned Christians

Wouldn't you think seasoned Christians ought to know better? I witnessed first-hand the mistreatment of people we consider different, independent thinkers, and who don't move to the same beat as others. If there is any such thing as being overly joyful, that was my husband's state of mind. He expressed, "I found a new family." Totally into the Word, my husband would rather study than eat. He sat for hours with his head in the Bible, speaking scripture passages out loud and marking up his Bible as well. He regularly attended Sunday worship and mid-week Bible Study. When he sang, it drove me crazy. He was not off-key, but the majority of the time he was a one beat behind, which made congregational singing awkward. His voice echoed over the sanctuary. Early on, Dallas demonstrated potential leadership skills. He was consistently willing to pray publicly, serve communion, zealous in the study, a consistent tither, and just a dedicated young servant. He was the epitome of a man wanting to do everything to show appreciation to Christ and his new family.

Dallas eagerly became a part of the Preaching Clinic Pastor J designed for men who wanted to sharpen their preaching skills and desired to deliver a trial message every fourth Sunday. One Wednesday following the midweek Prayer Meeting, Dallas and Pastor J were standing at the podium engaged in what looked like a serious conversation. I happened to sit on a pew a few feet away, yet close enough to hear a little of the conversation. Pastor confronted Dallas about my daughters calling him daddy. Dallas asked, "What's wrong with it?" Not wanting to appear meddlesome, I kept my head down. The prolonged conversation and Pastor's tone prompted me to

look up. Even though Dallas was slightly smiling,
disappointment was written all over his face. Pastor's
finger was pointed at Dallas's face a little too close;
sternly, he said, "Well then you don't preach." He then
walked off and left Dallas standing on the pulpit.

I was hurt for Dallas and, at the same time,
furious. He highly respected Pastor J.   Gradually, Pastor
J's disapproval of Dallas became evident. We didn't exist.
Some Sundays, Pastor's message was a mixture of the
Word and his personal opinion of our marriage. What is it
about Wednesday nights prayer meeting that will, at times,
turn into a gossiping session? Requests were made on
behalf of others, and with the same breath, all their business
was aired.   One particular Wednesday night, sarcasm was
aimed directly at us for the entire night. Others took notice,
but no one dared to speak against Pastor J. I got up and
went to the basement. One of the Sisters came down,

supposedly to console me, not knowing I knew she talked against us as well.

Dallas was stripped of his spiritual responsibilities. I knew it was just a matter of time and Pastor J would start working on me. He revoked my teaching and leadership privileges, directing the choir, etc. We had become isolated pew sitters. It all became a pattern of negative behaviors. Dallas grew tired, and he had enough. What was so sad is that Dallas's response was not in an aggressive way. After months of mistreatment, one Sunday following worship, Dallas took my hand and guided me to one of the back classrooms and said, "Brenda, we can't do anything here, I think its best that we leave." I felt the same way but didn't want it to be my decision. There was no alternative. Staying under that toxic atmosphere was not feeding our spirit. We transferred our membership to another congregation, although our hearts were back at North 35th Church.

I didn't realize it was happening, but it was the beginning of a mental meltdown for Dallas. Pastor's attitude crushed him, and over time negative feelings resurfaced. He was a man who, at the time, the congregation nor I knew he had a mental disorder. Dallas was a man who found new hope and thought the world of his family in Christ. And now this. My husband was secretively and desperately struggling to handle emotions he had tried to put to death.

Dallas became less talkative and aloof. His demeanor was no longer a look of confidence and contentment. The pressures of humiliation and put-downs were too overwhelming. His once optimistic views of the Church were scarred. The people he had envisioned as loving and caring were now his persecutors. On top of the mishaps, his mind became a playground for Satan. The hurt intensified the instability already in his mind.

People come to the church as broken vessels, and we make their lives worse. The Apostle Paul warns Christians to not become stumbling blocks. *"Woe unto you, scribes and Pharisees, hypocrites! for ye compass sea and land to make one proselyte, and when he is made, ye make him twofold more the child of hell than yourselves." Matthew 23:15 (KJV)*

This passage speaks to us today as well. Jesus is talking about Christians going to the extreme to convert a person, and because of our attitudes and traditions, we make them twice as bad as we are. How many people have we run away from the Church? How many people avoid the Church because we won't accept them as they are? It's like trying to gut a fish before you catch it. *"And now these three remain: faith, hope and love. But the greatest of these is love." I Corinthians 13:13 (NIV)* Without love we are like a tinkling cymbal, a sounding board. Love is the main thing; it leads to forgiveness.

Chapter 18

Power of Forgiveness

In the case of hateful words, assumptions, malicious gossip, misunderstandings, and deceptions, forgiveness has to be a line of attack. There are unrestricted walls of a forgiving spirit. The highlight of this book was credited to our inability and God's proficiency to enact forgiveness in me and my children. The outcome of the horrific and volatile trials gave evidence and confirmation of His supernatural power and the true meaning of forgiveness. The exact opposite of the fleshly nature is forgiveness, which transcends our instinctive nature to retaliate, to begrudge, and to take revenge on those who hurt us. Jesus had much to say about how we are to treat one another, even our enemy. He instructed us to do the opposite of our human instincts. In Jesus' culture, turning the other cheek meant not to retaliate revengefully using evil means.

Instead, we should do unto others as we would have them do unto us. *"On the contrary, repay evil with blessing," I Peter 3:9 (KJV)*

One problem with this verse is that in reality, people won't always treat you as you deserve or as you want to be treated. On the contrary, be aware not all people feel good or love themselves for a number of reasons. A healthy-minded person has high expectations, treats themself well, and in doing so, their expectations of how others treat them are also high. If I'm in love with myself, I won't intentionally do anything to harm myself and will limit what I allow others to do to me.

First Lady Michelle Obama was spot on when she said, '*When they go low, we go high,*' and it is a modern-day approach to any insulter. Jesus had in mind something more fulfilling, which is for us to operate in a spiritual realm, in a mind-frame beyond human capacity when we have been wronged. So, what do you do?

"Kindness used in the Bible means to be tendered hearted and is the good nature of love.

Many Christians who are good people tend to be unkind and critical. Kindness of love strives for fairness toward God and your fellow man. Kindness seeks the best for your fellow man, regardless of what he may do. In essence...requires loyalty, reliability, and both are born from the love of God. Kindness discards all bitterness and thoughts of revenge and emphatically endeavors to live in peace with everyone. Love that is kind <u>must</u> be a distinctive characteristic of Christ followers; only then will we succeed as witnesses. Our kindness must be evident to all people; they will then ask about the source of our kindness and so find Jesus." "Kindness Promises from God for Daily Living," *Christian Arts Gifts*, 2007, pg. 112.

"Those who are kind benefit themselves, but the cruel bring ruin on themselves." Proverbs 11:17 (NIV)

Forgiveness—The World's View

In general, people view forgiving someone as a weakness; however, that is far from the truth. To forgive is control and power devoid of haughtiness. To forgive is to inherently maintain control over human emotions. Forgiveness is an attribute, and like wisdom, I believe it is to be freely given for the asking. Testing to forgive comes through heinous trials, sins of commission, and the sins of omission. In and of us, the act to forgive is impossible to demonstrate. *"For God so loved the world that he gave his only Son that whosoever believes in him, shall not perish but have everlasting life. For God sent not his Son into the world to condemn the world; but that the world through him might be saved." John 3:16-17 (KJV)*

For substantiated sins, human weakness, and frailties that merited the stripes Jesus took, God turned his back on his only Child. His Son forgave and willfully gave His life for the entire world. Heartfelt, personal, and God-breathed are the opposition to the world's view of forgiveness. When this is understood, freedom becomes transparent and subsequently made clear to others who struggle with the idea. It wasn't until I became a Christian that I heard of the word forgiveness and the value of this attribute.

People are confrontational, will lie, dig pit holes, afflict unnecessary pain, manipulate, play mind games, and covet. This is the fallen world in which we live. Human behavior will challenge us to make a decision to forgive or not to forgive.

Desire It—Crave It

We have craving and desires we prioritize, and there is also a deep satisfaction in fulfilling these needs. We sweat, toil, and seldom allow anyone or anything to stand in the way of self-gratification. Simplifying it, many of our requests of God are for materialism, and like a spoiled child, we pout if God doesn't deliver. The spirit to forgive should be treated like any other human need or want.   Why aren't we motivated to put the same energy and drive into asking God to bless us with spiritual virtues? In my storm of matrimony, God showed me time and time again if I hold my peace in certain situations, He would show up in ways that freed my hand from making matters worse, bogging myself down with issues of which I had no control, and reminded me there is a Higher Power who can avenge better than I.

I recalled working at a school as an Assistant and one day while in the office for my evaluation with the Lead Teacher (my supervisor) and the Director. Based on comments the Lead Teacher made, which were not true, he denied me from getting a pay raise. I was furious. How quickly that little emotion called anger can flare up. I was hurt, and the tears were lingering, but I wouldn't let one drop fall. I wanted to punch the time clock and walk off the job.   Having every right to be agitated, common sense tapped me on the shoulder and reminded me I had three mouths to feed. Masking an angry countenance around the workplace, refraining from not putting forth my best efforts on the job, instead, I chose to forgive and move forward. To forgive is possessing waiting power to depend on God to deliver in ways we can't.

At the same school, I was an Assistant Instructor. In the absence of another Lead Teacher, I filled her position. A week turned into two weeks, then into a month. The Director, who was always what I called prowling around, would come to the classroom, stand in the door and, from time to time, compliment my classroom management skills. He would comment, "The curriculum is spot on. For once, the children's artwork is not looking the same…" Time passed, and the Lead Teacher hadn't returned. Confidentially, an employee of high rank and a reliable source revealed to me that the Lead Teacher had no intention of returning and was seeking employment elsewhere. Too much time had elapsed, and there was an immediate need to fill the permanent position of Lead Teacher. The Director, the same person who complimented me on my work ethics, had the audacity to decide to hire the Kindergarten Teacher who turned in her resignation months before my filling in for the Lead Teacher. The Director called me to his office and, with a sheepish grin, set me up by telling me what a great job I had done, and how calm and busy the students were, etc. Then came the letdown. He gave me his personal view as to why I was not a candidate for the position. Grieved and beyond disappointment, I left school that evening, went home, and talked to the Lord. The next day, I was determined and prepared to approach the Executive Director and make him aware of the situation.

To my surprise, the next morning, the Assistant Director and other colleagues had gone on my behalf to the Executive Director, who requested the Director to submit my resume and the Kindergarten Teacher's resume for his review. Following the review, the Director was instructed to call the Kindergarten Teacher to explain she was no longer a candidate for the position. When he called me to his office to tell me I had the job as Lead Instructor, of course, he had that sheepish grin and talked as if it was all his idea.

Unconditional love permeates compassion and forgiveness, which generates actions of good deeds under the most trying circumstances. God is the conscience of every man, at least He should be. Liberty and peace are in forgiving. We are His ambassadors and are to be lovers of man's souls. *Then came Peter to him, and said, Lord, how oft shall my brother sin against me, and I forgive him? till seven times? Jesus saith unto him, I say not unto thee, Until seven times: but, Until seventy times seven." Matthew 18:21-22 (KJV)*

"This meaning is behind the symbolism of the numbers. In the Bible, the number (7) symbolizes completeness or a finished work. The number 70 signifies perfect spiritual order carried out with all spiritual power and significance. Therefore 490 is a product of 70 x 7, signifying spiritual perfection of perfect order and completeness. Jesus' response to Peter was that forgiving completely wasn't good enough, but to forgive to the point of spiritual perfection." "The Symbolic and True Meaning of Seventy Times," *ChristianBlog.com*: Bullinger, 1921, p. 235.

The mathematical equation, *(70 x 7 = 490),* is symbolic of Jesus' expectations of how prevalent forgiveness is. For the duration of our life, we are obliged to practice the spirit of forgiveness. Now, does it mean we are doormats? Should verbal, emotional, and physical abuse relentlessly replay in our lives? Absolutely not. God is a God of order, justice, and composure. I believe He requires His children to be levelheaded as much as possible. Having our minds tranquil and our "thinking cap on" moves us in a direction to think about the culprit in a different manner, and to make a decision based on what Jesus would have us to do.

Horrific Examples of Forgiveness

February 26, 2012, in Sanford, Florida, United States, "George Zimmerman fatally shot a 17-year-old African American teenager by the name of Trayvon Martin. Trayvon's mother is part of a circle of mothers called MMTMF, Mothers Movement, Trayvon Martin's Foundation, a national network dedicating time and resources in assisting affected mothers of children killed by law enforcers. These mothers were special guests at the Democratic Convention/National TV Interview to share their pain and feelings regarding the deaths of their sons. What was impressive was Trayvon Martin's mother's profound statement, *"I am not saying I don't miss Trayvon walking around here on this earth, but God has shown me this is something bigger than me and that my son was sacrificed for a greater cause."* There was silence and tears as the mothers felt the same revelation. Trayvon's mother added to her statement, *"Forgiveness is a process. We are now in the process of forgiveness; we are not there yet..." Travon's Parents on the Path to Forgive George Zimmerman:* BBC.com, August 24, 2013: *Mothers of the Trayvon Martin Movement to Speak at the Democratic National Convention TV Interview*: July 26, 2016. The Martins turned a tragic situation into a positive and higher purpose.

On June 17, 201, in Charleston, South Carolina, Dylann Roof, a 21-year-old White male walked into a historically Black church during a Bible study service and killed nine people. He said, *"I was there to shoot Black people to start a race war."* At the first bond hearing, the Judge allotted time for each victim's family to speak.

Neither of the family members displayed anger as they calmly encouraged him, *"We're praying for your soul. Repent, confess, give your life to Christ, and change your ways. You'll be better off than you are now."* One of the victim's granddaughter's remarked, *"I forgive you. May the Lord have mercy on your soul."* " I Forgive You, Relatives of Charleston Church Shooting," *Washington Post:* June 19, 2015.

In reading these two concrete incidents, please don't get caught up in race. Both are illustrations of the <u>power to forgive a wrong that could never be made right</u>. God alone fixed the hearts of these souls and led the families toward humility and obedience to a Higher Power to withhold a grudge from someone who has victimized them. To lay aside personal hurt and allow <u>revenge</u> to be His. It is no little thing to be able to do this. The world calls it timid or feeble, but the Christians know it as *strength under control.*

In this world, we are like vulnerable lambs subject to evil forces. Apostle Peter of the Bible declared, *"Daily, we are like sheep ready to be butchered."* It is vital that we come to understand it has nothing to do with race, position, rank, educational status, politics, saved, unsaved, rich, or poor. We all are all fleshly inclined and are affected by one another.

Components Which Lead to Forgiveness

Prayer: In the midst of viciousness, repulsive actions, evil seen an unseen that are unreachable for us, but not for God, prayer works. The power of prayer and movement changes people and situations. Jesus prayed while clinging to the old, rugged cross, *"...Father, forgive them for they know not what they do..." Luke 23:34 (KJV).* Jesus' art of prayer demonstrated love and compassion to the masses, and He claimed we would do greater works. When we as the Body of Christ render forgiveness to our enemy, it manifests and magnifies God's character and unmerited favor on the entire world. The Bible asks us in I John 4:20 how can we claim to love God whom you haven't seen, but hate your brother or sister you see daily? And if anyone identifies with this, it further states we are liars, for God is love.

Jesus sat on the mountain near the Sea of Galilee, taught the Beatitudes, and alluded to forgiveness, mercy, and the blessings to be received when we exercise these attributes in everyday living. Blessed and happy are you.

Indifference: Forgiveness has no preference and will not show favoritism. Forgiveness is not reserved for relatives and friends. It is extended even to those who are *unfavorable, unlovable* from the layperson to the President and officers in the White House, whose faulty decisions, biases, personal perspectives, unfiltered statements, and ill-treatment have an effect on our lives. *"I urge you first that petitions, prayers and intercessions and giving thanks be made for all people, for Kings..." I Timothy 2:1-3 (NIV)*

Since we all human baggage, understand whether intentional or not, people will make mistakes and do wrong. However, change is a process. So, we exercise the ability to be patient with others until their change comes, thinking upon the patience God has shown to us down through ceaseless ages. He is merciful and patient while we clean up our act. Seize opportunities and teachable moments in the formative years before your children reach the age of accountability and teach them lessons on forgiveness. At a tender early age, if we teach their little mind and mouth to speak these important words, *"I forgive you"* and *"I am sorry,"* maybe forgiveness won't be so difficult for them in adulthood.

Extending Self

Jesus requires us to go a step further than just saying I forgive; the proof requires us to do and perform the unthinkable. *If your enemy is hungry, give him food to eat; if he is thirsty, give him water to drink. Proverbs 25:21*

(NIV) In the model prayer, Jesus teaches us to pray,
"...forgive us of our debts as we forgive our debtors."
Matthew 6:9-13 (NIV).

An informative read is *On the Up and Up* by Brenda Strone Browder. She tells a compelling story of marrying a man who failed to reveal he had a terminal illness (HIV) and was dying. Talk about forgiveness. Forgiveness is renewing a right spirit toward a person and not continuously reliving the sin or wrong toward you. Realistically, proximity may not be possible with some folks because the Bible tells us to be wise. It's like being in the presence of a snake and aware of its habits, and knowing it is venomous, you do what is necessary to safeguard yourself. Somehow, we can curse not and pray for the adversary to be delivered from their evil ways, and when coming face to face with the enemy, kindness can be shown.

Forgiveness isn't an emotion; it is a choice. It is a sound decision to release another person of a debt or an entitlement. Forgiveness is like having a debit card. I have ownership and the prerogative to use the card at my will. The guarantee of continuous use of the card is dependent on the dividends, what I have to gain when using my card. As long as I have the card and the money is in the account, I'm able to access the funds. When the choice to forgive presents itself, God is willing to supply the spiritual dividends of love, a liberated spirit, unexplainable joy, and above all, is having our sins forgiven if we are willing to forgive others. *"For if you forgive men their trespasses, your heavenly Father will also forgive you. But if you do not forgive men their trespasses, neither will your Father forgive your trespasses." Matthew 6:14-15 (NKJV)*

Last, but not of lesser importance, forgiveness is not for the person who did the wrong, but it is for us so we can be free. In order for God to develop a spirit of forgiveness within us, there has to be some opposition. In the scheme of life on a daily basis, there are colossal challenges that prompt us to make a choice to forgive. Here are some of my challenges, and perhaps you recognize some of them in your life.

Forgiveness is: Placing a great portion of my life on hold to raise my sister's children. Years pass with no thanks for the sacrifice, and I received poor treatment as if I were the villain. I am thankful that in 2018, I received an apology, thanks, and my sister and I have closed the door to the past.

Forgiveness is: When a family member's sexual curiosity takes control and results in having my grandchildren's removal from my home and handed over to the Cabinet for Children and Family Services.

Forgiveness is: Attending seventeen or more court hearings, fighting for my livelihood, job, and to clear my name. My spouse gave up and refused to support me financially and emotionally because he felt the Judge had the upper hand. Forgetting parts of his vows, *"for better or worse,"* and most imperative that God is both judge and jury, and He always has the final say.

Forgiveness is: Observing law enforcers use court meetings as a means of deception, falsifying data, and flat out lying. The Prosecutor and Case Workers were determined to take my job and end my career because I fought for justice, the rights of my grandchildren, and my career.

Forgiveness is: In the process of getting a Master of Education and being forced to resign or be fired from my teaching position because of an issue having nothing to do with the school system. Degraded, humiliated, and pushed to a level of numbness and unable to produce any more tears.

Forgiveness is: During critical times, living with the thought of family assumptions, "You have built a wall, and you act like you don't need anyone." They don't call and acknowledge my losses or ask if there is anything they can do to help.

Forgiveness is: My spouse becomes weary and decided life insurance is too much to carry, so he continues his policy but suspends mine.

Forgiveness is: Being physically violated and out of respect for another's reputation and family, I ponder the incident between God and me.

Forgiveness is: Behind my back, my stepson's mother is a playmate for my spouse.

Forgiveness is: Finding out from a college professor that my husband is on campus telling colleagues and staff, I am a lesbian.

Forgiveness is: My Christian walk is misinterpreted as being *"Holy than Thou."*

Forgiveness is: Unintentionally, nevertheless, I become a victim of my mother's actions because I look and sound like my mother, but I'm not her.

Forgiveness is: During a hospital visit with an older sister-in-the-Lord, she scolds me in front of another sister and my daughter. Her assumptions are based on my husband's perspective on marital problems. Respectfully, I wait until I get home to break down in tears.

Forgiveness is: Married, but 85% of the time I'm alone living life like a single woman.

Forgiveness is: When Church family is talking about my children and me as if we're invisible. While sitting in the midweek prayer meeting, a Deacon decided to ask prayer for my spouse. The Senior Pastor piggybacks off the requested prayer and says, "Your husband needs to stop fooling around with all these women around here."

Forgiveness is: My spouse asks me to go with him to witness to a friend. A couple from the Church decided to go along as well. While in discussion, in walks the lady's boyfriend, who candidly said to my husband, *"How are you going to call yourself a Christian when you were trying to kiss her?"* Candidates for the Church that day, I don't think so.

Forgiveness is: While in midweek Bible class, the Pastor subtly turns the entire class into a lecture about my marital situation. The tension is so thick I could cut it with a knife. Holding back unleashing a *"deadly poisonous tongue,"* I dismissed myself and retreated to the basement to regroup, followed by someone who I know has spoken against me and now comes to console me. Lord, deliver me.

Forgiveness is: Frequently riding three buses to work in mid-January and freezing weather. I started an hour in advance to wake up my spouse to drive me to work, and he lies there unresponsive.

Forgiveness is: Using every ounce of strength and energy to juggle school, career, family, ministry, and myself while Satan's darts are fired at me from all angles. Yearning for a little support, I find my soul mate is throwing a few darts too.

Forgiveness is: My children are grown and occasionally tend to forget all that I've been through to care for them.

Forgiveness is: Helping to repay two extensive loans that were taken out without my knowledge or consent.

Forgiveness is: Living with an idol, an enemy, in my home that called 'sleep.' I faced 'sleep' the first thing in the morning before leaving for work, and 'sleep' is the first thing I saw when I returned home because 'sleep' dominated my spouse.

Forgiveness is: The Christmas holiday came and went, and my spouse showed up two weeks later, justifying his absence with, "I spent Christmas with my mother."

Forgiveness is: Having a conversation with my adult children, who ask about their father allegedly being sexually intimate with a relative. That's like being struck in the face with a brick. After confronting my husband, he gave me the silent treatment. Then on another occasion, my daughter bluntly maintained her daddy had been with a relative. A few years after my divorce, I was going through my ex-husband's things in preparation for his move to a new facility. I came across a letter addressed to him that confirmed the sexual intimacy and who it was with. To this day, the relative is not aware that I know of the infidelity.

Forgiveness is: Withstanding the haters. People who carefully observe my faith, perseverance, and endurance as I move forward during troublesome times. People who can't quite figure out why I am blessed despite the hell in my life. People who misconstrue my circumstances, hoping my situation will be my fall.

My story is not so much about overcoming struggles with schizophrenia, as it is allowing the Holy Spirit to develop fortitude in me and my children and to let God work on our behalf. That is the ***power of forgiveness.***

"...the God of all comfort, who comforts us in all our troubles, so that we can comfort those in any trouble with the comfort we ourselves receive from God. 2 Corinthians 1:3-4 (NIV).

*****

In the Appendix at the end of this book, I have included additional information about forgiveness. There are questions and answers, scriptures, and a journal. I encourage you to take the time to read and work through those pages as well.

Chapter 19

Schizo-Hilarious

Laughter is a coping mechanism.

Laughter is healthy, therapeutic, and relieves tension. What helped me through some trying times is when I focused and ponder on incidents and comments Dallas made after the fact. Then and only then could I laugh about it. Occasionally, Dallas and I joked and laughed about the illness and medicine. I would tease him by saying, "Dallas, if you don't take your medicine, I am going to call the paddy wagon to come to get you." He and I would crack up laughing.

Over the years, when Dallas seldom smiled, or it seemed he had lost the ability to smile, it was exuberating when laughter filled the room and refreshing when I could once again see his white teeth. I want to caution, there is a difference between laughing with and laughing at, between poking fun, and seeking to bring out the humor in the person or a situation. A smile, a small gesture of laughter can be a special moment for someone who struggles to keep their sanity or takes life too seriously. Learn to find humor, and maybe the next time the person does or says something, you'll find it less disturbing or perhaps deal with the situation differently. What I'm attempting to say is that in dealing with mental illness, it doesn't all have to be gloom and doom.

My entire family found Dallas to have a unique character and sense of humor that made us laugh with him. When we discussed the issues amongst ourselves, he could laugh as well. I can assure you laughter was helpful to Dallas's spirit, although short-lived. Sometimes things with Dallas were just plain ludicrous. I'm glad we took the time to laugh and find moments of humor that I found to be "schizo-hilarious." Here are a few of those moments I just had to share about the lighter side of Dallas.

Fun Times with Dallas

It was typical for Dallas to have an enormous accumulation of garbage. Aaron was cleaning his apartment, and he gathered seven bags of garbage. As Aaron was taking the bags out the door, Dallas grabbed the bags and yelled, "This is my garbage!" Really Dallas— your garbage?

Dallas took our children and their friends skating, and when he returned to pick them up, he entered the doorway of the rink, stood with his hands in his pockets, and yelled louder than the sound of the music, *"Kni-jel. Ta-me-ka. Mar-cy.* His voice vibrated over the entire rink. The kids quickly learned the drill, which was to return their skates and be at the door as fast as possible. He got away with this a few times before they learned to look out for him and eliminate further embarrassment.

I purchased some men's body wash for Dallas, and he said, "Where did you get that body wash? It smells good. I like something that you can wash up with, and you don't have to put anything else on. I still use Dawn dishwashing liquid to take a shower so that I won't use up all the body wash." Really Dallas?

While Knijel and her daddy were shopping at Walmart, they ran into Woody, a brother in Christ who was an employee. After greeting one another, Woody walked off to go back to work. Dallas stood in the middle of the floor and yelled as though making a public announcement on a loudspeaker, "Woody, I'm glad you're not in the streets anymore." Knijel said, "Daddy, don't be so loud." Of course, Dallas's favorite words were, "I was just encouraging him."

Darlene, a sister in Christ, took the police to Dallas's condo so they could do a wellness check. Dallas was laid stretched out on the couch, hands folded across his chest, staring at the ceiling. Sternly he said, "Darlene, you better get out of here with those policemen, or you are going to be in trouble. You are going to the lake of fire."

One day while driving down Shelbyville Road, suddenly I heard various voice tones, "DXL, Oxmoor Center, Chick-fil-A, Outback, Dance studio, Stein-Mart, Office Depot, Catherine's, Moby Dick, a whale of a fish, Farmer's Market, they use to have some good food, Thornton's Gas Station," From high pitches, drawn-out, monotones, and ad-lib sounds, Dallas read every billboard, tagline, and store sign along Shelbyville Road. We had miles to go before getting home, and he was still on a row. Have you ever heard a song and it stayed in your head for the rest of the day? Well, you can only imagine what I heard after we got home.

Dallas placed a bottle of red fruit punch in the refrigerator and accidentally left the top loose. The punch dripped from the refrigerator on to the kitchen floor. Whenever we came over, the juice was still on the floor, so

I said, "Dallas, you need to mop up that juice. Bluntly, he said, "I am. I am. I need to get some Soft Scrub with Clorox first." I explained, "Dallas, the Dawn dish liquid and a little water will wipe up the spill or either call housekeeping to clean the floor." Dallas, "Nah. Nah. I'll get it. I need to get some Soft Scrub with Clorox first." Oh my God, he's like a needle stuck on a record playing the same tune over and over.

Dallas badgered my daughter for days to take him to Walmart to purchase a clock and more household items. He wasn't in the store over twenty minutes before deciding he didn't want to purchase any extra items, just an alarm clock. Once at check-out, Dallas decided not to purchase the clock; he complained, "This line is too long. I'm going to put this clock back. Knijel replied, "No, Daddy, we are going to get that clock, we didn't come to this store for nothing." Dallas got out of line and went to the next cashier and loudly asked the customers, "Hey, can I get in front of yaw? Holding up the clock, he continued, "I only have this one thing."

Dallas was going apartment hunting, and I was cool with that, but the problem for me was the straggly wild hairs sticking out all over his face and food particles stuck in his beard and mustache. So, I said, "Dallas, you need to shave off some of that beard because food is getting stuck there; either you are not aware of it, or you don't care. Plus, you have food all over your clothes." He responded, "Nah, I'm alright. I need to look like I'm homeless if I need a place to live."

We had just picked up some fast food, and because Dallas was driving. He felt I ought to feed him his French fries. Not that I would have minded putting a fry or two in his hands, but he took it a step further and said one of his past girlfriends would have fed him. I came back with, "I'm not one of your girlfriends."   He then comes up with something totally irrelevant to the conversation, saying,

"I'm a new creature," without thinking, I said, "You're no damn new creature." He burst with laughter. I was not amused.

My nephew, Damon, came to visit us. Dallas showed Damon his written tablet of Black Tae Kwan Do and offered to show him some moves. Dallas dropped into a bent-knee stance and began moving his arms back and forth with clinched fists. Damon looked at his glassy eyes, determined face, and stood still because he saw his Uncle was serious about taking him down. Dallas was not too pleased with my nephew's response to his moves, so anxiously, he said, "Damon. Come on, man." Damon politely bowed out and later told me, "I know some Karate too, and I wasn't going to let Uncle Dallas use his full force on me." Smart thinking Damon.

Dallas and I discussed the irritableness, neuropathy, and how irritating the nerve itch was. He said, "I used to wear a black leather jacket, black pants, and steel toe boots and allowed myself to itch. I was disciplining myself to fight. I thought that I was going to have to fight the Communist."

One Wednesday evening during Bible study, Dallas strolled in the sanctuary wearing a long sleeve print shirt wrapped around his head, with one sleeve hung down in front of his face between the dark black shades which covered his eyes. Wouldn't you know it, he sat on the pew right beside me.

Dallas's Brother, Dennis, and I drove him to the VA hospital. While waiting in the emergency area, Dallas was moving as if he was on a child's seesaw, up and down, up and down, while making quite a few weird sounds. Dennis, a little intimidated and embarrassed, looked up at Dallas and dropped his head. Beside Dennis was a table with *Reader's Digest* magazines on it. He picked up a magazine and handed it to Dallas. Dallas held the magazine over his head, opened his mouth wide, and chuckled like a child who had just received a new toy. He then tossed the Readers Digest into the air and continued his creepy movements. Dennis dropped his head. Inwardly, I cracked up.

Dallas has called me on the phone, and when I didn't answer, he'd leave a message. "Hey woman, it's me." He would leave four or five different messages, each at least five minutes or longer on the voicemail, and each ended with, "Call me, woman!" Other times Dallas called my phone, and after a long conversation, I would say, "Dallas, I have to go." *(Silence)* "Well, I have one more question." He would ask the question and began another conversation. Me again, "Dallas, I have to go." *(Silence)* "Okay." and he continued to talk, "I love you, Brenda; you take care of yourself. Uh. What you think you'll be doing tomorrow? What time do you think you'll get up tomorrow? Me, "I'm not certain, Dallas, I have to go." "Okay. You take care of yourself, and I love you. Be careful, and God be with you. Okay, bye. Be careful, take care of yourself, God be with you. *(Silence)*. He would then ask, "Are you still there? Me, "Dallas, you have to *hang* up!" "Take care of yourself, God be with you." At times he would hold the phone and say, "Brenda, you have to hang up."

Dallas rambled on about different gods and although I told him there isn't but one God, he proceeded to speak of these gods, 'Amen Raw', a Black god; the god of all gods; 'Ghor' god of war, 'Buford' his guardian angel; 'Max Killer-Ah-Brew' a soldier with multiple personalities that could win every war, and he didn't let anybody down; 'Rafar' a Black god who distributed created power to everyone including his children who he had control over." At one point, I asked him why didn't Rafar give power to his wife, and he explained, "He didn't give her any power because she might do something evil." He asked, "Do you want me to tell you about the other ones?" Politely I said,

"No Dallas, I've heard enough." Dallas was a terrible speller, yet he created the spelling for each one of these gods.

Knijel was cleaning Dallas's apartment and attempted to open a box of garbage bags that I had purchased prior to him moving into the new place. Dallas yelled at her, "No, Knijel, don't open those garbage bags. Those garbage bags are sentimental; your mother bought those for me."

One Thanksgiving Day, our oldest daughter, Tameka, decided to take Dallas and me out for dinner. Grudgingly, while deciding I uttered a small request, "Lord, God, whatever he does or says, give me a quiet spirit." The Lord knows there are days I can handle Dallas, and others, I just lose it when his schizophrenia is evident. After we got home from dinner, Tameka told me she had called her Aunt and said, "I am taking Momma and Daddy out for Thanksgiving dinner and you know he has a way of pushing Momma's buttons. It's Thanksgiving, let them act up, and I'm leaving them both at the restaurant."

It was always a pleasure to hear Dallas use his gift of prayer with one exception. His tone was so tranquil, and he began every prayer with, "Father God, Lord Jesus, Sweet, Holy Spirit." One Sunday morning, Pastor Johnson asked Dallas to lead the opening prayer. Dallas prayed, and prayed, and prayed while the entire time-shifted his feet back and forward. Some of the youth turned, stared, and smiled at our son Aaron. Poor thing.

Dallas, the girls, and I would kneel and pray before bedtime. I would peek over at Dallas heavily into prayer. I gently touched Tameka and Knijel, and we quietly left him right there on bended knees.

The family gathered in the upstairs dining room for Thanksgiving dinner. I wanted to boost Dallas's esteem, and so I asked him to pray over the meal. A quick second, I thought, oh no. I had to call his name to get his attention.

I don't know for sure, perhaps it was the tone I used when I called out his name or whatever because the family burst into laughter. Everybody knew what time it was. We wanted to eat dinner on Thanksgiving Day. Dallas looked up and laughed. Apparently, Dallas knew he had gotten carried away and forgot about dinner.

In all things, try to find some humor.

Chapter 20

The Woman I Am Today

The fable entitled: *The Tortoise and the Hare* is a story of two creatures in a race. The value of time is one of many lessons to be gleaned from the fable. As the story goes, the hare was overly confident in his skill to be faster in the race since the tortoise was of a slow nature. Feeling the upper hand in winning the race, the hare decided he could take time to rest and fell asleep. The analogy is, in life we can take for granted we have much more time to spare when in reality, time waits on no one and is not confined. Time can either pass swiftly or drudgingly like the tortoise and move slowly.

Twenty-seven years of marriage appeared to have doubled. Life can make one feel as if trapped in a straitjacket, and the more you struggle for release, the more powerless you feel. Seconds, minutes, days, weeks, months, and years seem to creep when life is beating up on you. Consequently, there were periods when my struggle with Dallas's schizophrenia seemed to drift. The longevity of trials positioned me to either cope or fold under pressure. I felt cheated of marital pledges and promises. Expectations of him as a Christian man were shattered. The mutual bond and spirituality we once shared were broken by negative invasions, fleshly nature, and constant interruptions. Internal shadows invaded what I thought was a "marriage honored by God." The marriage tried my relationship with the Lord and tore at my faith. It tested my faithfulness, trust, and how dependent I was on God. This marriage challenged whether my true discipleship would hold fast under the pressures. Gold must go through a process in order to remove the impurities before its true value is actually seen. Tunneling through years in the marriage, I became aware of how the spiritual process molded, shaped, and transformed me to a higher level of spiritual maturity and refined me to a state of my best self. I believed there are tailor-made trials for each of us and spiritual growth and faith are contingent on the trials we face.

In a conversation with Dallas, I spoke the following words, "You may not have been good for me, but I was good for you." The truth be told, he was good for me too. Not so much as a husband, but because the schizophrenia and his weaknesses brought me face to face with spiritual wickedness in high places. I faced off with who I was and who I could further become with the power of the Holy Spirit. I observed strength and a level of passion in me that I never knew I possessed. I grew to understand what the Apostle Paul meant when he said, *"I glory in my infirmities, for in my weakness by the grace I am made strong."* When I asked God to take away something as devastating and hurtful as what I was going through, I learned to accept when He said no, wait, or move on and to be okay with His decision.

I have to pause here and say whenever trouble arises in a marriage, it's an open door and an opportune moment for Satan to deter the mind of the hurting spouse. He seizes the time he can entertain adultery, especially if one partner has already broken that vow. I am thankful that no matter what took place, I held fast to my morals and didn't make any decision that would be hard for me to live down. Marriage to Dallas strengthened my convictions, morals, and developed eternal attributes that are priceless such as perseverance, steadfastness, endurance, wisdom, and more. *"But they that wait upon the LORD shall renew their strength; they shall mount up with wings as eagles; they shall run, and not be weary; and they shall walk, and not faint." Isaiah 40:31 (KJV).* This particular scripture was a significant help, for I meditated upon it often, and it became one of my favorite passages.

"Persecuted, but not forsaken; cast down, but not destroyed; Always bearing about in the body the dying of the Lord Jesus that the life also of Jesus might be made known in our body." 2 Corinthians 4:9-10 (KJV). "What, then, shall we say in response to these things? If God be for you who can be against us?" Romans 8:31 (NIV)

Dallas remains an important part of our family. Every now and then, he would share his inner thoughts, letting me know he loves us and, most important, appreciates us withstanding the strongholds of schizophrenia. For example, these are just a few things he has spoken from his heart. "If I had the mindset then, that I have now... If you all would just forgive me... All that you have done all these years... The kids love me, they need me, and I need them. I know why I married you. You know how you can be so blind that you just can't see what others see? I have regrets, and I just have to suffer the consequences. I hope I go before you. The world won't be the same without you. *"*

One thing for sure, he never elaborated much on was his military experience. His voice took on a tone of sadness as he shared his affirmation for serving in the Army, "I was never so disappointed…" It was the first time I heard Dallas express feelings of anguish over losing the privilege to serve in the military. This could have been part of his anger with himself. I felt empathy for him. At some points, I needed a tap on the shoulder or a little reminder to help me move past his inconsideration and mood swings to use patience with his emotional inconsistencies, delusional thoughts, and radical behaviors.

Now I deal with Dallas from a distance, and I remain conscious about allowing myself to revisit the past. Apostle Paul wouldn't allow the past to interfere with the pursuit of the new, a relationship with Jesus Christ. He left the past where it belonged, behind him, and pressed on toward a higher calling in Christ Jesus.

In Dallas's rational state of mind, God is definitely the center of his thoughts. He testifies of his grace and how had it not been for God, he doesn't know where he would be. This is why we should be careful not to write anyone off. Our frail minds are clueless as to how God works in and through others to work His plan of salvation. God can use even a mentally ill person as a witness and make a change in the world. In marriage with Dallas, and because of what I was dealing with, I had to stretch beyond my train of thought and many times was faced with this discernment. God, what is the purpose of Dallas being in my life? *"For my thoughts are not your thoughts, neither are your ways my ways, saith the LORD." Isaiah 55:8 (KJV)*

I don't know what your shadows are. Whenever they hover over you, the key is how you decide to handle them. A second flawed marriage, unbearable changes, and pain inflicted upon my children all played a part in the existence of who I am today and the capability of being open about my story being read by many. God bless the hands that pick up this book. Prayerfully the words of each page will be connective, transparent, informative, inspirational, and supportive. God covered me with a renowned peace. Marriage to Dallas was an experience that made me the woman I am today.

APPENDIX

Forgiveness Questionnaire

How are you standing with forgiveness? The following fourteen questions on forgiveness were written, and permission is given by Father Al Lauer Presentation Ministries, Priest, Lauer, Al Father: www.presentationministrities.com - 2016.

1) What is forgiveness?

Forgiveness is our decision to accept God's grace to let go of the hurt due to sin committed against us and to express this by acts of mercy and love toward the offender (see Luke 15:20-24).

"Forgiveness is the restoration of freedom to oneself. It is the key held in our own hand to our prison cell" (Pope John Paul III).

2) How often must I forgive?

70 x 7. That is always indefinitely, always. (Matthew 18:22)

3) **Are there any sins committed against me for whom I don't have to forgive**?

No. The Lord calls us to forgive all sins.

4) **When I forgive, am I condoning sin?**

No. The Lord forgives all our sins and condones none of them.

5) **Must I forgive the person offending me if he/she isn't sorry?**

Yes. 'For' is before 'give' – which means to give pardon before being asked for forgiveness, or even if never asked forgiveness.

6) **Must I forgive if a person continues to hurt me?**

Yes. While hanging on the cross, Jesus forgave His enemies (see Luke 23:34).

7) **If I forgive a person, do I stay in an abusive situation?**

No. You free yourself to obey God and remove yourself from an abusive situation until it is changed.

8) How do I forgive?

None of us can forgive by our own power. "To err is human, to forgive is divine, and we are not divine."

9) What if I don't want to forgive?

We should pray and ask the Lord to change our hearts.

10) How quickly must I forgive?

Immediately. (Matthew 5:25) We're in a self-made jail and at a stand-still in our relationship with God until we forgive.

11) What if I forgive and not forget?

Forgetting offenses against us does not mean we have amnesia, but there is no special sting.

12) How do I forgive myself?

The Bible does not speak of our forgiving ourselves. Not forgiving ourselves is a symptom that will take care of itself if we truly forgive others and receive prayers of healing.

13) What if I don't forgive?

1. We "give the devil a chance to work on" us (see Ephesians 4:27).

2. We are handed over to tortures (fear, lowliness, depression, frustration, anxiety, and self-hatred. (Matthew 18:34).

3. We cut ourselves off from receiving forgiveness (Matt. 6:12, 15), healing prayer (Mark 11:25), worship (Matthew 5:23-24), and the Christian community.

4. We lose our appetite for prayer, the scriptures, and small and mass Christian fellowship. We become spiritually anorexic.

5. If we persist in unforgiving, we cut ourselves
   off from God forever and thereby damn
   ourselves.

14) How do I know if I have forgiven?

Forgiveness is not a feeling; it is a decision.

Forgiveness Personal Growth Journal

List brief details and dates when you exercised the power of forgiveness.

1. _____
   _____
   _____
   _____

2. _____
   _____
   _____
   _____

3. _____
   _____
   _____

4. _____
   _____

5. _____

_____

_____

6. _____

_____

_____

7. _____

_____

_____

8. _____

_____

_____

9. _____

_____

_____

10. _____

_____

"Father, forgive them for they know not what they do."

Luke 23:34 (KJV)

Scriptural Journey

❖ *Isaiah 40:31(NIV) "But those who hope in the LORD will renew their strength. They will soar on wings like eagles; they will run and not grow weary; they will walk and not be faint."*

❖ *Ephesians 6:13 (NIV) "Therefore put on the full armor of God so that when the day of evil comes, you may be able to stand your ground, and after you have done everything, to stand." New Translation says, "Then after the battle you will still be standing firm.*

- ❖ *Philippians 4:13 (NIV) - "I can do all things through Christ the One who strengthens me."*

- ❖ *Psalms 46:1 (NIV) - "God is our refuge and strength, an ever-present help in trouble."*

- ❖ *I Corinthians 15:58 (KJV) -"Be ye steadfast, unmovable, always abounding in the work of the Lord that you know that your labor in the Lord is not in vain."*

- ❖ *Psalms 34:1 (KJV) - "I will bless the Lord at all times; His praise shall continually be in my mouth."*

- ❖ *Romans 8:31(KJV) - "What shall we say to these things? If God be for us, who can be against?"*

- ❖ *Romans 8:28 (KJV) - "And we know that all things work together for the good of them that love God, to them who are called according to his purpose."*

- ❖ *Romans 8:37 (KJV) – "...We are more than conquerors..."*

❖ *II Timothy 2:15 (KJV) - "Study to shew thyself approved unto God, a workman that needeth not to be ashamed, rightly dividing the word of truth."*

❖ *I Peter 5:6-7 (KJV) - "Humble yourselves therefore under the mighty hand of God that he may exalt you in due time: Casting all your cares upon Him for He cares for you."*

❖ *II Corinthians 4:9-11(ESV) – "We are hunted down, but never abandoned by God, knocked down, but not destroyed..."*

❖ *Revelation 22:7 KJV) - "Behold, I come quickly; blessed is he that keeps the sayings of the prophecy of this book."*

Women of Inspiration

Rahab – A harlot who trusted God by word of mouth, was saved and became a part of the lineage of David. *Joshua Chapter 2*

Ruth – Pagan woman who learns to love the God of her mother-in-law. Her legacy: *"Where you go, I shall go; your people shall be my people, and your God shall be my God,"* How many of us are willing to give up family for God? *Book of Ruth*

Mary, the Mother of Jesus – Young. Devoted. The ability to ponder and hold her tongue. *Luke Chapters 1 and 2*

Anna – Prophetess prayed and asked God to spare her life to see the King, Baby Jesus. *Luke 2:36-38*

Mary, Sister of Lazarus– Understood there needs to be balance in her life. She knew when to sit down and listen to the words of Jesus. *Luke 10:38-42*

Deborah – Courageous prophetess, warrior, and a judge who gave glory to God for the victory over their Canaanite oppressors. *Judges Chapters 4 and 5*

Esther – Courageous and bold. Risked her life to go before the King on behalf of her people, Israel. *Book of Esther*

The Woman with the Issue of Blood – Possessed enough FAITH to drag her ailing body to Jesus to be healed. *Matthew 9:20-22*

Proverbs 31 – The Virtuous Woman – Lemuel's mother instructs him in how to find a good wife. *"Her children will rise up and call her blessed."*

We Cry

God, the Creator of Humanity.

Father, from day to day, I don't know how my life

will unfold.

Help me to be aware of your presence in life's

uncertainties.

I express my soul and release my pain; liberate me

from strongholds.

I stretch toward Thee and place my hand in yours.

Holy Spirit make me victorious.

Lead me into everlasting life with You, Father,

Son, and Holy Spirit.

Lord I cry unto thee, not for myself only, but for all

who hope in Your Son

Amen.

Brenda L. Moore

Lessons I've Learned

_____

_____

_____

_____

_____

_____

_____

_____

_____

_____

_____

About the Author

Brenda L. Moore is a native of Louisville, KY. She is a former Teacher of Interdisciplinary Early Childhood Education for twenty-five years for Jefferson County Public Schools / Saint Joseph Children's Home and Child Development Center.

Brenda earned a Master of Education, Bachelor of Science in Education, and an Associate degree in Christian Education. Her passion for Teaching prompted her to be a Substitute Teacher for the courses Conflict Resolutions / Teaching Methods at Simmons College of KY and to be the lead teacher of God's Woman Class at the College of the Scriptures, Louisville, KY. Brenda served as Social and Program Director for the College of the Scriptures and Danville Community College, Danville, IL.

Brenda is a Christian mother, grandmother, and great grandmother whose loyalties are love and devotion for her Lord and Savior, to family, and the service of people. Twenty-seven years she endured mental illness which gave her the incentive to become a first-time author of "Walking in the Shadow of a Schizophrenic / Power of Forgiveness."

Brenda has a joy for the work of the Church and has served in the various capacities: Bible Teacher, Chairperson of Women's Ministry, Sunday School Superintendent, Youth Advisor, Program Director, Chairperson of Missions, Choir Director, and Christian Camps.

Her motto is, teach children while they are young and they will cope with most of life's experiences. Her future aspirations and goals are to advocate for women and to use her book as a teaching tool for group discussions in mental health facilities.

Thank you so much for reading this book and I greatly appreciate your support.

Please feel free to leave a comment or review on Amazon.com, Barnes & Noble.com or email us at blm.221955@gmail.com.

Made in the USA
Columbia, SC
28 June 2021

41054297R00196